"In a moment where Islamaphobia has been normalized in U.S. schools, Dr. Noor Ali pushes us to challenge assumption and stereotype. Her efforts stand as a critical, practical and unapologetic commitment to keep Muslim students safe while reminding them that they are seen and cared for."
        David Stovall, *Ph.D., University of Illinois at Chicago*

"In *Creating Inclusive Classrooms for Muslim Students*, Noor Ali masterfully weaves essential insights into the school experiences of Muslim students together with action recommendations deeply informed by those insights. The result is a transformative vision for equity, for something more than little tweaks and equity optics. If you're ready for that transformative vision, do yourself a favor and read this book; if you're not ready for it, do yourself an even bigger favor and read this book."
        Paul Gorski, *Co-author with Seema Pothini of* Case Studies on Diversity and Social Justice Education

"As we fiercely engage as changemakers, in anti-oppression work, Dr. Ali's comprehensive guide is a must-have tool to ensure our focus is inclusive of Muslim students and all students, waiting to be acknowledged. Courageous educators are pivotal in dismantling oppressive systems and I encourage everyone to use this book, as you guide your work, everyday."
        Michelle Chalmers, *MSW, Racial Justice Educator, White People Challenging Racism? Moving from Talk to Action*

Creating Inclusive Classrooms for Muslim Students

Creating Inclusive Classrooms for Muslim Students: A Practical Guide for Teachers is the first comprehensive resource specifically designed to help K-12 educators understand and address the unique educational experiences of Muslim students. Drawing on Muslim Critical Theory (MusCrit), this book translates complex theoretical concepts into immediately actionable classroom strategies.

The book explores six core tenets through real classroom case studies spanning elementary, middle, and high school contexts: recognizing systemic oppression, addressing the impact of visible Muslim identity, acknowledging gender intersections, amplifying authentic Muslim voices, challenging white cultural norms, and fostering essential allyship. Each chapter provides reflective practice exercises, concrete implementation strategies, and comprehensive resource lists.

Readers will gain specific tools to recognize anti-Muslim bias in curriculum materials, create culturally responsive classroom practices, support students with visible religious identities, and advocate for systemic change. The book transforms good intentions into effective practice, ensuring Muslim students can thrive authentically in your educational spaces.

Noor Ali is an Associate Professor at Northeastern University's College of Professional Studies, Graduate School of Education where she teaches undergraduate, graduate, and doctoral students. Dr. Ali serves as the Concentration Lead for Transformative School Leadership in the Ed.D. Program at Northeastern University. She is author of *Counter-narratives of Muslim American Women: Creating Space for MusCrit*.

Equity and Social Justice in Education Series
Paul C. Gorski, Series Editor

Routledge's Equity and Social Justice in Education series is a publishing home for books that apply critical and transformative equity and social justice theories to the work of on-the-ground educators. Books in the series describe meaningful solutions to the racism, white supremacy, economic injustice, sexism, heterosexism, transphobia, ableism, neoliberalism, and other oppressive conditions that pervade schools and school districts.

Integrating Educator Well-Being, Growth, and Evaluation
Four Foundations for Leaders
Lori Cohen and Elizabeth Denevi

Humanizing Pedagogies with Multilingual Learners
Transforming Teaching in the Content Areas
Kara Mitchell Viesca and Nancy L. Commins

From Empathy to Action
Empowering K-6 Students to Create Change Through Reading, Writing, and Research
Chris Hass, Katie Kelly, and Lester Laminack

Promoting Equitable Math Instruction
Exploring Elementary Teachers' Stories
Monica L. Gonzalez and Alesia Mickle Moldavan

The Social and Emotional Core of Equity Leadership
A Guide for Driving Change in Schools
Gianna Cassetta

Creating Inclusive Classrooms for Muslim Students
A Practical Guide for Teachers
Noor Ali

Creating Inclusive Classrooms for Muslim Students

A Practical Guide for Teachers

Noor Ali

Routledge
Taylor & Francis Group
NEW YORK AND LONDON

Designed cover image: © Getty Images

First published 2026
by Routledge
605 Third Avenue, New York, NY 10158

and by Routledge
4 Park Square, Milton Park, Abingdon, Oxon, OX14 4RN

Routledge is an imprint of the Taylor & Francis Group, an informa business

© 2026 Noor Ali

The right of Noor Ali to be identified as author of this work has been asserted in accordance with sections 77 and 78 of the Copyright, Designs and Patents Act 1988.

All rights reserved. No part of this book may be reprinted or reproduced or utilised in any form or by any electronic, mechanical, or other means, now known or hereafter invented, including photocopying and recording, or in any information storage or retrieval system, without permission in writing from the publishers.

For Product Safety Concerns and Information please contact our EU representative GPSR@taylorandfrancis.com. Taylor & Francis Verlag GmbH, Kaufingerstraße 24, 80331 München, Germany.

Trademark notice: Product or corporate names may be trademarks or registered trademarks, and are used only for identification and explanation without intent to infringe.

ISBN: 978-1-041-01191-0 (pbk)
ISBN: 978-1-003-61360-2 (ebk)

DOI: 10.4324/9781003613602

Typeset in Palatino
by Newgen Publishing UK

To Muslim youth: May you find spaces where you can be and become yourselves and not have to explain yourselves.

Contents

Acknowledgments ....*xv*
Meet the Author..*xvii*

1 Understanding Muslim Experiences in Education 1
   Introduction 1
   From Theory to Practice: MusCrit in K-12 Education 4
   Why MusCrit Matters for All Educators 5
   How to Use This Practical Guide 5
   The Journey Ahead 6
   A Final Ask 7

**2 Understanding Systemic Patterns in
   Educational Settings** 8
   Introduction 8
   Framing our Conversation 11
   Reflective Practice 12
   Putting it into Action 13
     *Case Study 1: Confronting Colonial Legacies at Eastview
        Elementary 13*
     *Case Study 2: Confronting Security Discourse at Westfield
        Middle School 16*
     Case Study 3: The Day Democracy Died in Room 237 20
   Classroom Strategies and Activities 22
     Strategy 1: Historicizing Muslim Presence in America 22
     *Strategy 2: Analyzing Security Discourse in Educational
        Contexts 24*
     *Strategy 3: Addressing Geopolitical Contexts of Muslim
        Experiences 24*
   School-Wide Implementation 25
     Conducting Institutional Archeology 25
     Transforming Institutional Discourse 26

Conclusion 27
Resources for Teachers and School Leaders 28
  Academic and Research Resources 28
  Digital Rights and Surveillance Resources 28
  Curriculum Resources on Civil Rights and Security 29
  Organizations Supporting Civil Rights 29

3   Navigating Visible Religious Identity at School 30
Introduction 30
Framing our Conversation 33
Reflective Practice 34
Putting it into Action 35
  Elementary: The Books Started It All—Ms. Rivera's 3rd Grade Journey 35
  Middle School: They're Watching Us, Right?—Identity Navigation in Mr. Hall's Classroom 37
  High School: Literature as Liberation—An English Teacher Confronts Surveillance Culture 39
Classroom Strategies and Activities 41
  Strategy 1: Normalizing Visible Muslim Identity in Classroom Culture 41
  Strategy 2: Building Student Agency Around Identity Expression 43
  Strategy 3: Addressing Intersectional Dimensions of Muslim Identifiability 44
School-Wide Implementation 46
  Creating a Culture of Religious Respect and Accommodation 46
  Visual Representation 47
Conclusion 47
Resources for Teachers and School Leaders 48
  Identity Development and Expression Resources 48
  Classroom Resources for Supporting Religious Identity 48
  Literature Featuring Identifiable Muslim Characters 48
  Classroom Management Resources for Identity-Based Incidents 49

Contents ◆ xi

**4 Understanding Gender and Faith in Student
Experiences** 50
Introduction 50
Framing our Conversation 53
Reflective Practice 54
Putting it into Action 56
  Case Study 1: Elementary School: The Ripple Effect 56
  Case Study 2: Middle School: The Perfect Storm 57
  Case Study 3: High School: The Masterclass 60
  After Class: The Visiting Teacher's Questions 61
Classroom Strategies and Activities 63
  *Strategy 1: Reframing Gender Narratives in Your
    Curriculum 63*
  Strategy 2: Creating Dialogue Spaces for Exploring Gender 64
  Strategy 3: Gender-Conscious Classroom Practices 65
School-Wide Implementation 66
  Policy Advocacy Through Demonstrated Need 66
  Strategic Family Partnerships 66
Conclusion 67
Resources for Teachers and School Leaders 68
  Academic and Professional Development Resources 68
  School Policy and Implementation Guides 68
  Books Featuring Diverse Muslim Gender Experiences 68
  Digital and Online Resources 69
  Community and Support Networks 69
  Curriculum and Classroom Materials 69

5 Amplifying Counter-Narratives 70
Introduction 70
Framing our Conversation 73
Reflective Practice 73
Putting it into Action 75
  *Current Event Case Study: Civic Education Through
    Contemporary Counter-Narratives 75*
  Elementary Teacher Story: The Journal Project Revolution 76
  *Middle School Subject-Specific Approach: Science Class
    Redefined 77*
Classroom Strategies and Activities 79

*Strategy 1: Critical Media Analysis: Unpacking Dominant
    Narratives 79*
  *Strategy 2: Counter-Narrative Immersion: Beyond Token
    Representation 80*
  *Strategy 3: Student Voice Studio: From Analysis to
    Creation 81*
  School-Wide Implementation 82
    Teacher-to-Teacher Influence 82
    Student Leadership as Cultural Catalyst 83
  Conclusion 84
  Resources for Teachers and School Leaders 84
    Academic and Professional Development Resources 84
    Curriculum and Classroom Materials 85
    School Policy and Implementation Guides 85
    Books Offering Muslim Counter-Narratives 85
    Digital and Online Resources 85
    Community and Support Networks 86

6 **Examining Cultural Norms in Educational
  Environments** 87
  Introduction 87
  Framing our Conversation 89
  Reflective Practice 91
  Putting it into Action 92
    Elementary: The Names We Carry 92
    Middle School: The Palestine Exception 93
    High School: The Professional Academic 94
  Classroom Strategies and Activities 96
    *Strategy 1: Challenging Language Hierarchies: From Deficit to
      Asset 96*
    *Strategy 2: Rethinking Assessment: Beyond White Western
      Demonstration 97*
    *Strategy 3: Integrating Islamic Intellectual Traditions Across
      the Curriculum 98*
  School-Wide Implementation 98
    Teacher-Led Cultural Audits 99
    Collaborative Knowledge System Revision 100
  Conclusion 100

Resources for Teachers and School Leaders 101
   Academic and Professional Development Resources 101
   Curriculum and Instructional Resources 101
   School Policy and Implementation Guides 102
Resources for Students 102

7 The Essential Role of Allies 103
Introduction 103
Framing our Conversation 105
Reflective Practice 105
Putting it into Action 106
   Elementary Case Study: When Good Intentions Go Wrong 106
Middle School Case Study: The Bathroom Revolt 108
   High School Case Study: The Walkout That Wasn't 111
Classroom Strategies and Activities 115
   Strategy 1: Everyday Moments of Solidarity 115
   Strategy 2: Interrupting Harm with Courage 116
   Strategy 3: Leveraging Privilege for Systemic Change 117
School-Wide Implementation 118
   Creating Institutional Protection in Hostile Climates 118
   Navigating Resistance While Sustaining Allyship 120
Conclusion 122
Resources for Teachers and School Leaders 123
   Academic and Professional Development Resources 123
   Curriculum and Instructional Resources 123
   School Policy and Implementation Guides 123
   Resources for Students 124

Conclusion: The Work That Remains 125
What We've Learned, What We Face 126
The Resistance You'll Face 126
The Urgency of This Moment 127

Appendix A: Your Personal Journal 128
Where Are You Now? A MusCrit Self-Assessment 128
   Recognizing Systemic Oppression 128
   Addressing Identifiability 128
   Acknowledging Gender 129

Amplifying Counter-Narratives 129
　　　Challenging Whiteness as Norm 129
　　　Fostering Essential Allyship 130
　　Quick-Start Implementation Checklist 130
　　　This Week I Will: 130
　　　This Month I Will: 130
　　　This Semester I Will: 131
　　　This Year I Will: 131
　　Questions for Deep Reflection 131
　　　About Your Practice: 132
　　　About Your Students: 132
　　　About Your Community: 132
　　　About Yourself: 133

Appendix B: Classroom-Level Audit Tool 134
　　School-Wide Audit Tool 138
　　　Instructions 138
　　　School Climate and Culture 138
　　　Curriculum and Instruction 139
　　　Staffing and Leadership 139
　　　Family and Community Engagement 139
　　　Student Support Services 140
　　　Assessment and Accountability 140

　Bibliography　　　　　　　　　　　　　　　　　　　　　*143*

Acknowledgments

This work exists because of the countless Muslim students who trusted me with their stories—in classrooms, during interviews, in quiet moments when no one seemed to be listening. You showed me what it means to navigate impossible choices daily. Every page of this book carries your voice.

My gratitude also to every teacher who has made space for Muslim youth—who learned that Ruqayyah means "rise like the sun," who created corners for prayer, who stood up when others stayed silent. You are doing work that changes lives and letting your Muslim students believe that they do belong.

Dr. Paul C. Gorski, series editor for Routledge's *Equity and Social Justice in Education* series—thank you for understanding why this work matters and for helping shape a platform where Muslim student experiences can finally be centered. Lauren Davis, thank you for your partnership in making this vision a reality.

When I first developed MusCrit, I had no idea it would become what it has. The community of Muslim scholars who have taken this framework and made it their own, who have pushed it further than I ever imagined, and built a collaborative that isn't just an academic space, is proof that we can carve out room for ourselves in places that weren't designed for us. We've built this together. The Muslim scholarship that stands behind me and ahead of me has chosen to refuse silence.

To my friends and colleagues who believed in this work before it was fully formed: you saw the potential when I was still finding my voice. Thank you for not letting me make myself small. To the mentors who pushed me to claim space and time for this work when I was still introducing myself as "originally from Pakistan." You taught me that my voice matters exactly as it is. I wish everyone has someone like you.

To Adnan, Maahin, Momin, and Amal: you've lived with this book as much as I have. Maahin and Momin, watching you grow into young Muslim men who refuse to make themselves small has taught me more than any research ever could. Amal, the way your face lights up when you see yourself in a story reminds me why this work can't wait.

To my ancestors who refused to let their stories be silenced, who carried their faith through diaspora, across oceans and borders, and wrapped us always in their duas—you taught me that our voices are inheritance, and that speaking truth is the legacy we honor.

And to the Muslim youth who will hold this book—may you find teachers who see your brilliance, classmates who celebrate your differences, and schools where you can be and become yourselves without explanation.

And most importantly, Alhumdulillah!

Meet the Author

Dr. Noor Ali is an Associate Professor at Northeastern University's Graduate School of Education and the Concentration Lead for Transformative School Leadership in the Ed.D. Program. As the developer of Muslim Critical Theory (MusCrit), a groundbreaking theoretical framework within Critical Race Theory, Dr. Ali has carved out essential space for understanding the lived experiences of Muslim Americans in educational settings.

Born in Lahore, Pakistan, and educated across two continents, Dr. Ali brings a unique perspective to her work bridging theory and practice. A veteran K-8 educator, former Principal and current strategic lead to pilot the high school at Al-Hamra Academy in Shrewsbury, Massachusetts, she has spent over two decades in classrooms, developing innovative approaches to inclusive education. Her daily work with Muslim students and families informs her research on creating educational environments where all students can thrive authentically while contributing their voices to our collective learning.

Dr. Ali is the author of *Counter-narratives of Muslim American Women: Creating Space for MusCrit* (Brill, 2022) and the poetry collection *One Teaspoon of Home: Desi Food Poetry* (Markings, 2023). Her scholarship has been featured in leading education journals. Dr. Ali has spearheaded the creation of the Critical Muslim Education Research Special Interest Group at the renowned AERA. She presents regularly at national conferences on topics of educational equity, social justice, and the Muslim

American experience, developing what she calls an Equity-Informed Framework for creating inclusive classrooms.

Beyond her academic work, Dr. Ali serves as a Commissioner for the New England Association of Schools and Colleges (NEASC) and was elected as a Trustee to the Shrewsbury Public Library. She has been actively involved in diversity, equity, and inclusion initiatives at both institutional and community levels, including serving on Shrewsbury's DEI Taskforce.

Dr. Ali holds a Doctorate in Education from Northeastern University, with previous graduate work in Inclusion Education and English Literature.

Dr. Ali currently resides in Shrewsbury, Massachusetts, with her husband and three children. She continues to advocate for systemic change in education while mentoring the next generation of educators and leaders. Her work bridges the academic and the personal, offering educators concrete, research-backed tools for creating more inclusive and equitable learning environments where Muslim students and all students can flourish.

1
Understanding Muslim Experiences in Education

Introduction

When Sarah sneaks into the quiet end of the hallway under the staircase to offer her afternoon prayer, heart pounding in case someone spots her there, or when Zakaria says he prefers to be called Zach when he really doesn't, or when Mariam notices the absence of a moment of silence at her school after the loss of Muslim life in a hate crime in her city, or when Usman skips lunch because there were no halal options and the cafeteria also ran out of salad, or when Rania requested an excused absence for Eid, but state testing was also scheduled for that day, it is not just a minor inconvenience. It is a proclamation of othering. A statement that you are less than, that you are irrelevant, on the sidelines, unseen, an inconvenience that will require an accommodation, and therefore a recipient of benevolence from a system not obligated to serve you.

In the landscape of American education, the pursuit of equity and inclusion remains one of our most pressing challenges. As our classrooms become increasingly diverse, educators are called upon to create learning environments that not only acknowledge, but also actively support the full range of student experiences. Among these diverse voices are those of Muslim students, a population that has faced unique and intensifying challenges in recent decades, particularly as global events have left Muslim students navigating experiences of marginalization, surveillance, and direct oppression within their educational communities.

The need for targeted approaches to supporting Muslim students has never been more urgent. Recent data from the Council on American-Islamic Relations Massachusetts (CAIR-MA) reveals that 48% of Muslim students reported being bullied for being Muslim during the past school year. Among female respondents who wear the hijab, 35% experienced physical harassment at school, including incidents of having their hijabs pulled or removed. Muslim students repeatedly share how school administration avoids or silences concerns related to their educational experiences. These statistics reflect the daily reality of students who must navigate educational spaces while managing assumptions, stereotypes, and many times hostility related to their religious identity. The examples I shared above and those that follow in the book are all centered on the true shared experiences of Muslim students in America.

Yet despite these documented challenges, most educators lack specific frameworks for understanding and addressing the complex ways that religious identity becomes racialized in American schools. Traditional diversity approaches, while valuable, often miss the particular mechanisms through which Muslim students experience marginalization and these generic inclusion strategies may inadvertently overlook the unique intersection of religion, race, politics, and identity that shapes the Muslim American experience.

This work emerges from the intersection of my lived experience and scholarly inquiry. As a Muslim woman who has navigated American educational spaces as both student and educator, I don't approach this work from a distance. I've lived these dynamics while also studying them systematically.

I remember being in college, finding an empty classroom to pray in and keeping the lights turned off so I wouldn't get caught praying. I've sat in doctoral seminars introducing myself as "originally from Pakistan" when what I meant was that I'm Pakistani-American, realizing only later how I was sanitizing my identity for a predominantly white audience. I've watched my son jokingly call himself Kevin in high school because our names are considered "difficult." I've also stood in professional spaces where my brown opinion mattered less, where representation was invited but voice was not. I've navigated the exhausting work of being the Muslim educator expected to speak for all Muslims while simultaneously having either my religious or academic authority questioned when I do speak.

But I've also experienced the profound impact of allies, with friends who check in on us, walk in protests, or the teachers who created space for students to pray without hiding. I've seen how one inclusive book in a classroom library can transform a child's relationship with their identity, how my own daughter's eyes light up when she sees a Muslim name in a storybook, and how authentic counter-narratives can dismantle years of internalized stereotypes.

This positioning, as both researcher and community member, shapes every page of this guide. When I write about systemic oppression, I'm drawing from data and experience from the daily navigation of educational spaces as a visibly Muslim woman. This isn't theoretical, it's the texture of my professional and personal life. Therefore, the urgency behind this work isn't academic either; it's deeply personal and profoundly communal. Every Muslim student who has learned to make themselves small, every family navigating impossible choices between authentic expression and social acceptance, every educator who has witnessed harm but lacked frameworks for addressing it—they are why this work exists.

When you implement these strategies, you're not just applying pedagogical techniques. You're participating in the essential work of creating educational spaces where Muslim students can be fully themselves while contributing their authentic voices to our collective learning. You're helping ensure that no child has to pray with the lights off or introduce themselves as less than they are.

From Theory to Practice: MusCrit in K-12 Education

Three years ago, I developed Muslim Critical Theory (MusCrit) as a theoretical framework to understand the complex experiences of Muslim Americans in educational settings. Building on Critical Race Theory's foundational insights about systemic racism, MusCrit examines how religion becomes raced when a population is categorized based on characteristics like clothing, names, accents, or country of origin, reducing individuals to one aspect of their identity and creating new forms of racialized oppression. The framework also centers on a crucial insight: due to the racialization of religion and an assigned groupness, the Muslim American experience is often perceived as monolithic, when in reality the lived experiences of Muslim students represent a rich intersectional tapestry. These students continue to experience oppressive inequities ranging from microaggressions and invalidation to outright actions of violence, bigotry, and discrimination, patterns that traditional educational approaches have struggled to address effectively.

MusCrit's six tenets emerged from extensive research over the last decade, with Muslim American students and educators, revealing patterns that traditional frameworks couldn't fully capture:

- How historical, political, and social forces create systemic oppression against Muslims
- How visible markers of Muslim identity create unique vulnerabilities and navigation strategies
- How gender intersects with Muslim identity to shape different experiences
- How authentic counter-narratives by Muslims challenge dominant stereotypes
- How whiteness functions as the unmarked norm that marginalizes Muslim ways of being
- How essential allyship can create meaningful change for Muslim students

While my previous work established MusCrit as a theoretical framework, this book translates that theory into practical, actionable strategies for K-12 educators. You don't need to have read my earlier theoretical work to benefit from this guide. What you do need is a willingness to examine your assumptions, learn from Muslim students and communities, and commit to creating more inclusive educational environments.

Why MusCrit Matters for All Educators

The imperative for this work extends far beyond serving Muslim students alone. It is essential that the lived realities of all our students remain central to our educational practice. Avoidance is akin to silence, invalidation, and oppression. Meeting the needs of Muslim students, recognizing and acknowledging their experiences not as afterthoughts or accommodations, but as integral to creating authentic belonging remains critical to our broader mission as educators. Research consistently demonstrates that inclusive educational practices benefit all students, not just those from marginalized groups. When educators implement MusCrit principles, they: (a) Prepare students for a diverse world by fostering critical thinking about difference and similarity; (b) Challenge stereotypes and misconceptions that limit all students' understanding; (c) Foster empathy and inclusivity that creates stronger classroom communities; (d) Enhance cultural competence that serves educators throughout their careers; and (e) Address intersectionality in ways that support multiple student identities.

How to Use This Practical Guide

This book is designed as an immediately actionable resource for K-12 educators across all subjects, grade levels, and school contexts. Whether you teach in a diverse urban district or a predominantly white suburban school, whether you have many Muslim students or few, MusCrit principles provide frameworks for creating more inclusive and responsive educational environments. You will notice that each chapter follows a consistent, user-friendly structure designed to move you from reflection to implementation:

Introduction and Framing our Conversation: Each chapter begins with an introduction to the broader context and a personal vignette. An essential background on theoretical foundations and current research provides the knowledge base to understand why these issues matter and how they manifest in educational settings.

Reflective Practice: We begin with questions and scenarios that help you examine your own assumptions and experiences, not for judgment, but for honest self-assessment that creates space for growth.

Case Studies: Throughout each chapter, detailed examples from elementary, middle, and high school settings show MusCrit principles in action and help you envision implementation in your own context.

Think About It! Sections: Regular reflection prompts help you process learning and connect it to your specific teaching situation.

Classroom Strategies: The heart of each chapter offers practical, tested approaches that you can adapt to your specific context. These strategies come from real teachers working with real students.

School-Wide Implementation: This section prompts you to think beyond the classroom to the larger school community and how incremental change can become both deeper and broader.

Resources: Each chapter concludes with carefully curated materials for continued learning, including books, articles, organizations, and classroom materials.

The Journey Ahead

The six chapters that follow will equip you with specific tools and strategies for implementing each MusCrit tenet in your educational context. In Chapter 2: Understanding Systemic Patterns in

Educational Settings, you will come across tools for identifying and addressing patterns of discrimination beyond individual prejudice, with strategies for examining curriculum, policies, and school culture. Chapter 3: Navigating Visible Religious Identity at School, offers you approaches for supporting students with visible Muslim identity markers, creating spaces where religious expression is respected rather than targeted. Chapter 4: Understanding Gender and Faith in Student Experiences will provide you with nuanced strategies for understanding how gender intersects with Muslim identity across the spectrum of gender expression while Chapter 5: Amplifying Counter-Narratives focuses on incorporating authentic Muslim voices and perspectives across your curriculum. Chapter 6: Examining Cultural Norms in Educational Environments will emphasize the need for creating culturally pluralistic environments that value diverse forms of knowledge and expression, and lastly, Chapter 7: The Essential Role of Allies, centers our attention on building coalitions and support networks that sustain inclusive practices.

A Final Ask

Creating educational environments where Muslim students can thrive requires moving beyond tolerance toward true inclusion, building spaces where religious diversity is valued as an asset rather than managed as a challenge. This work demands courage, curiosity, and commitment to ongoing learning. The students in your classroom, Muslim and non-Muslim alike, deserve educational experiences that prepare them for our complex, interconnected world. They also deserve to see themselves reflected in their learning materials, to have their questions welcomed, and to develop critical thinking skills that will serve them throughout their lives.

2
Understanding Systemic Patterns in Educational Settings

"People have told me to go back home. I only know how to be American; I've lived nowhere else."—Rida

Introduction

For more than a decade I asked my middle school students this question: How do you feel about 9/11?

One important thing to consider is that I asked this question in a safe affinity space, where they were all Muslim, where they didn't have to worry what the answer would sound like, or how they would come across. Where no further explanation would be required.

I found that 99% of my students said they felt guilty.

Another, more important thing to consider is that each one of them was born after 9/11.

How is it that these children came into the world carrying guilt for something they had nothing to do with?

How is it that the expectation they cater to is one in which they have to explain themselves, rather than be or become themselves?

How does a 6-year-old or a 16-year-old navigate living with this burden, how does she move through classroom, content, and conversation, when she must first worry about how she appears, or the amount of discomfort her presence is causing in public educational spaces?

We begin by acknowledging the systemic nature of racialized oppression against Muslims, which is situated in specific historical, political, and social inequities unique to the Muslim experience. Unlike other forms of oppression based primarily on race or ethnicity, the Muslim experience involves a complex racialization of religion that transforms religious identity into a category for discrimination. This process has deep historical roots, is embedded in powerful political structures, and manifests itself through distinct social mechanisms that collectively create a hostile system of inequity.

Muslims exist within a paradoxical space in the American imagination—simultaneously hypervisible through security discourse and invisible within positive representations of American identity. This paradox stems from a centuries-old framing that positions Islam as fundamentally incompatible with Western values, an incompatibility that became particularly politicized in the post-9/11 landscape. As Selma, a Muslim student observed, "I was born after 9/11 but feel guilty about it. I would get the stares in the classroom when 9/11 was talked about."

This assertion of collectively guilty by association reveals how deeply embedded anti-Muslim sentiment is within American institutions, including educational spaces. When Muslim students must apologize for or distance themselves from acts committed by individuals with whom they share no connection beyond a religious category, we witness a unique manifestation of racialized religious oppression.

The racialization of Muslims exists regardless of their race and is positioned around stereotypical markers of "groupness", where a population is categorized based on characteristics such as clothing, name, accent, or country of origin (Garner & Selod, 2014). Religion is raced when these characteristics translate into an individual being seen through the lens of a singular facet of their identity, resulting in Muslim Americans experiencing hostile scrutiny when they have identifiable Muslim signifiers (Amrani, 2017).

The educational implications of this systemic oppression are profound. The CAIR-MA 2025 bullying report found that 48% of Muslim students reported being bullied for being Muslim during the past school year, while 35% of Muslim students reported that teachers or staff made offensive comments about Islam or Muslims. These statistics speak of a system that goes beyond individual prejudice to institutionalized practices and norms that systematically disadvantage Muslims. The transformation of Ahmed Mohamed's engineering curiosity into a criminal threat showed us how systemic racialization operates in schools. When the 14-year-old brought his homemade clock to MacArthur High School in Irving, Texas, his teacher saw not student innovation but potential terrorism. Within hours, Ahmed was handcuffed, fingerprinted, and processed through juvenile detention (CNN, 2015). This 2015 incident foreshadowed an escalating pattern: by 2025, Tufts doctoral candidate Rumeysa Ozturk faced deportation for co-authoring an opinion piece, with Secretary of State Marco Rubio declaring, "We gave you a visa to come and study and get a degree, not to become a social activist" (NPR, 2025).

What makes the Muslim American experience particularly challenging is the legitimization of anti-Muslim sentiment through national security discourse and foreign policy decisions. When educational institutions uncritically adopt security frameworks, Muslim students find themselves in the impossible position of having to prove their "American-ness" while navigating stereotypes of inherent foreignness. A Muslim student, Hafsa, shared, "Every time there's a mass shooting, I immediately pray it's not a Muslim" because the repercussions of any act of violence being perpetrated by someone who can be connected to a Muslim identity are great on Muslims where they are a minoritized population.

Here's a common refrain in my work with Muslim youth—they feel "we are considered not American enough." This sentiment captures the painful reality that regardless of birth, citizenship, or cultural practices, Muslim Americans are often positioned as perpetual foreigners, their American-ness always in question. Another participant shared, "I only know how to be American, I've lived nowhere else." Yet despite this reality, the pervasive nature of systemic oppression means that Muslim students are constantly required to prove their belonging, to justify their presence, and to explain their faith; burdens not placed on their non-Muslim peers.

This chapter explores how educators can recognize and address these historical, political, and social dimensions of Muslim oppression within educational settings. By understanding the specific contours of anti-Muslim racism rather than treating it as identical to other forms of discrimination, educators can develop more effective approaches towards equitable practices.

Framing our Conversation

Understanding the systemic oppression of Muslim Americans requires us to consider the ways in which historical forces, political structures, and social dynamics have created a unique form of racialized religious discrimination.

Anti-Muslim sentiment has deep historical roots in Western discourse that positioned Islam as fundamentally incompatible with Western values. Said's (1978) analysis of Orientalism demonstrated how this created seemingly natural associations between Muslims and characteristics like violence or irrationality, regardless of individual realities. Later, the post-9/11 political landscape intensified these dynamics by transforming religious identity into a security concern. Kundnani's (2014) concept of radicalization discourse shows us how Islamic religious practice became viewed as potentially threatening, while Puar (2007) demonstrates how the "Muslim terrorist" figure became central to reconstituting American identity itself.

These historical and political forces operate through social mechanisms that racialize religion, creating what Rana (2011) terms "racial panic"; heightened reactions that justify extraordinary scrutiny of ordinary Muslim behaviors. In schools, this manifests when student prayer triggers security concerns or when curriculum content about Muslim cultures prompts community complaints about promoting Islam.

Reflective Practice

Addressing the historical, political, and social foundations of Muslim oppression requires educators to engage in deeper forms of reflection that go beyond general cultural awareness. I recommend beginning by examining how your understanding of Muslims and Islam has been shaped by the political and media landscape of the post-9/11 era. Consider how the War on Terror framework has influenced educational approaches to discussing Islam, Muslims, and regions with significant Muslim populations. Do you find yourself more vigilant about certain behaviors from Muslim students?

You can also reflect on how international conflicts and U.S. foreign policy toward Muslim-majority countries might affect your Muslim students' experiences in educational spaces. When discussing global events in classroom settings, do you consider how Muslim students might feel when their family's countries of origin are framed primarily through lenses of terrorism, authoritarianism, or women's oppression? Do you create space for perspectives that challenge dominant geopolitical narratives about Muslim-majority regions?

Consider how historical misrepresentations of Islam and Muslims in Western educational traditions might influence your curriculum and teaching. Do your curriculum materials present Muslim civilizations as having contributed primarily to the medieval period but little to modernity? Also, examine how your school's policies and practices might reflect institutional biases against Muslims. Do security protocols disproportionately scrutinize Muslim students? Are disciplinary practices applied equitably, or do implicit biases result in different treatment of Muslim students, particularly boys who might be perceived as threatening due to stereotypes?

✅ Putting it into Action

Case Study 1: Confronting Colonial Legacies at Eastview Elementary

Eastview Elementary serves a diverse student population from immigrant communities, with about 12% Muslim students primarily of Bengali, Pakistani, and Somali backgrounds. The school is in a northeastern city with a history of industrial decline and revitalization through immigration. The school's journey towards inclusivity began when fifth-grade teachers Julie Chen and Marcus Washington attempted to implement a new district social studies curriculum on American Beginnings that presented a triumphalist narrative of colonial settlement with no mention of the nation's Muslim heritage.

Ms. Chen and Mr. Washington noticed how this curriculum positioned their Muslim students as perpetual newcomers to America despite the fact that Muslims have been part of American society since the colonial era, with an estimated 10–15% of enslaved Africans being Muslim. They brought their concerns to Principal Diana Rodriguez, who recognized this as an opportunity to address a deeper pattern of historical erasure affecting Muslim students' sense of belonging.

Dr. Rodriguez established a Curriculum Review Committee including teachers, the literacy specialist, the district curriculum coordinator, local historians, and representatives from various cultural communities including Muslim parents and community leaders. The committee's assessment went beyond merely auditing for representation to examining the conceptual frameworks underlying the curriculum—how was "American identity" defined? Whose experiences were centered? How were immigration and religious diversity framed?

Their assessment revealed patterns that reflected broader national narratives: American history was presented as beginning with European settlement; religious diversity was framed primarily through Christian denominational differences; immigration narratives positioned certain groups (particularly those from Muslim-majority countries) as perpetually new regardless of their historical presence; and contemporary units on citizenship emphasized assimilation to dominant cultural norms rather than examining how these norms developed through contested historical processes. Rather than simply adding Muslim content to this problematic framework, the committee worked with the district to fundamentally reconceptualize the social studies curriculum. The revised curriculum, Many Beginnings: Diverse Histories of American Communities, examined how different communities have become part of American society through various historical processes including indigenous presence, forced migration through slavery, voluntary immigration, refugee resettlement, and territorial expansion.

A key innovation was the development of a fifth-grade unit on Early Muslim Americans that examined the presence and contributions of Muslims during the colonial and early national periods. Students studied the stories of enslaved African Muslims like Omar Ibn Said and Ayuba Suleiman Diallo, whose Arabic writings have been preserved in American archives. They examined how these individuals maintained their religious practices under brutal conditions and how their Muslim identity shaped their experiences of American slavery.

Family and community engagement strengthened implementation through several initiatives. A Community Historians program invited family and community members to share historical knowledge about their communities' American experiences. These oral histories became part of classroom resources, helping students understand history as living knowledge held within communities rather than simply information in textbooks. A History Detectives family program engaged students and their families in investigating traces of diverse communities in local historical sites and archives.

Challenges included resistance from some district stakeholders who perceived the curriculum revisions as politicizing American history. The committee addressed this challenge by grounding their work in historical scholarship, emphasizing that the revised curriculum actually provided a more accurate and comprehensive understanding of American development rather than a political agenda. They also emphasized how the curriculum aligned with state standards for historical thinking, including analyzing multiple perspectives and evaluating historical evidence.

 **Think About It!**

Situation Analysis:

1. How does the original curriculum's erasure of Muslim American history reflect broader patterns in how American identity has been constructed through education?
2. What specific historical misconceptions might contribute to contemporary perceptions of Muslims as perpetually foreign to American society?
3. How might this historical erasure differently affect Muslim students from various backgrounds (Black Muslims, immigrant Muslims from different regions, converts)?

Implementation Analysis:

1. Evaluate the school's decision to fundamentally reconceptualize the curriculum framework rather than simply adding Muslim content to the existing framework. What makes this approach more effective for addressing systemic oppression?
2. How did the "Community Historians" program challenge traditional hierarchies of historical knowledge? Why is this approach particularly important for communities whose histories have been systematically excluded from formal academic study?

Alternative Approaches:

1. What if the school had addressed historical erasure primarily through supplementary activities rather than core curriculum revision? What limitations might this approach have?
2. How might a comparative approach examining the historical treatment of various religious minorities in America have enhanced or modified the implementation?
3. What additional considerations would be important in a school with significant historical tensions between different minority communities?

Application Exercise:

You are a third-grade teacher at Eastview Elementary preparing to teach a unit on your local community's history. Your district-provided materials focus exclusively on European immigrant contributions, despite your city having a historically significant Muslim community dating back to the early 20th century. Develop a curricular approach that:

- Incorporates local Muslim history without treating it as separate from the community's core development
- Uses age-appropriate methods to help young children understand historical presence and contributions
- Engages community resources and knowledge
- Addresses potential concerns about changing history or political correctness

Case Study 2: Confronting Security Discourse at Westfield Middle School

Westfield Middle School serves approximately 800 students in grades 6–8 in a predominantly white suburban community with a small but growing Muslim population (about 6%) primarily from South Asian and Middle Eastern backgrounds. The school's initiative began after a series of troubling incidents following an active shooter drill. Several Muslim students reported that during the post-drill discussion, classmates had made comments suggesting that Muslim students were more likely to become shooters. Additionally, a Muslim student who had been experiencing anxiety was reported to administrators after writing about feelings of alienation in an English assignment, triggering a security assessment protocol despite no evidence of threatening behavior.

English teacher James Harrison brought these concerns to Principal Stephanie Wong, who recognized that these incidents reflected how post-9/11 security frameworks were shaping perceptions of Muslim students. She established a Civil Rights Review Team including administrators, counselors, security personnel, teachers from various departments, the district's legal counsel, Muslim parents, and civil rights advocates from the wider community.

Rather than treating these as isolated incidents requiring only disciplinary responses, the team conducted a systemic review of how security discourse operated within the school. They examined discipline records, security protocols, threat assessment procedures, and bullying reports through a civil rights lens. They also interviewed Muslim students about their experiences navigating school security practices and perceptions and the review revealed deeply concerning patterns: Muslim students, particularly boys, were subject to heightened scrutiny from both peers and staff; security concerns were more readily triggered by Muslim students' behaviors that would be considered normal for other students; and the school's "See Something, Say Something" campaign had inadvertently created a climate where Muslim students were disproportionately reported for typical adolescent behaviors like expressing feelings of alienation or social criticism.

Based on these findings, the team developed a comprehensive approach addressing security practices, classroom discourse, and student support. The security component included revising threat assessment protocols to include explicit consideration of potential bias in reporting and evaluation. Security personnel received specialized training on distinguishing between actual warning signs and behaviors that might trigger concern due to implicit bias. The team also implemented regular civil rights reviews of security incidents to identify potential patterns of discriminatory implementation.

The counseling department developed a Belonging and Security initiative addressing the relationship between emotional safety and physical safety in school communities. This program helped all students understand how feeling targeted or unwelcome affects their sense of security, while also addressing how prejudice often masquerades as safety concerns. Counselors received specialized training on supporting students experiencing discrimination-related trauma, with particular attention to the impacts of security profiling on Muslim students' psychological well-being.

Challenges can include resistance from some stakeholders who perceive civil rights considerations as potentially compromising security which can be addressed by emphasizing that effective security depends on community trust and that discriminatory practices actually undermine safety by damaging this trust.

Think About It!

Situation Analysis:

1. How did post-9/11 security discourse specifically impact Muslim students at Westfield Middle School? What historical and political developments shaped these impacts?
2. Why might security frameworks be a particularly important aspect of systemic oppression to address for Muslim students compared to other marginalized groups?

3. How did the school's approach recognize the distinction between individual bias and systemic patterns in security practices?

Implementation Analysis:

1. Evaluate the Civil Rights Review Team's composition and approach. How did including legal counsel, security personnel, and civil rights advocates create a more comprehensive analysis than would have been possible with only educators?
2. How did the Student Civil Rights Team structure empower Muslim students while not placing the burden of education or advocacy solely on them?

Alternative Approaches:

1. What if the school had addressed these incidents through anti-bullying frameworks rather than civil rights and security analysis? What limitations might this approach have had?
2. How might explicit engagement with geopolitical issues affecting Muslim communities have enhanced or modified the implementation?
3. What additional strategies might be needed in a school where security discourse is particularly dominant, such as those with regular police presence or extensive surveillance systems?

Application Exercise:

You are a school counselor at Westfield Middle School. A Muslim student has been referred to you because teachers are concerned about his withdrawal and antisocial behavior after he stopped participating in class discussions following an international terrorist incident that received extensive media coverage. The referral notes mention security concerns despite no evidence of threatening behavior. Develop a response approach that:

- Supports the student's well-being
- Addresses the inappropriate security framing with referring staff
- Creates appropriate educational opportunities from the situation
- Connects to the school's broader civil rights initiatives

Case Study 3: The Day Democracy Died in Room 237

Amara sat frozen as her government teacher asked the class to debate whether enhanced surveillance of Muslim communities was justified for national security. Around her, classmates argued about whether Muslims could be trusted, whether mosques should be monitored, whether her family's mosque was a breeding ground for extremism. When she finally spoke up, her voice shaking, to say that surveillance made her family afraid to attend Friday prayers, her teacher interrupted, "Let's try to keep our personal feelings out of this and focus on policy." Later, a classmate approached her locker, "Why do you always have to make everything about being Muslim?"

That afternoon, Amara went home and told her parents she was dropping AP Government. "I can't keep pretending my existence is a debate topic," she said. Her father, who had immigrated from Syria twenty years earlier and become a U.S. citizen, sat quietly for a long moment. Then he said something that surprised her, "Maybe it's time we stopped being quiet."

What happened next broke every rule about how change is supposed to work in schools.

Instead of forming committees or conducting assessments, Amara's father called other Muslim parents. Instead of waiting for administrative approval, they organized. Within two weeks, fifteen Muslim students across different grade levels had documented their experiences of political exclusion in classrooms. Jamal, a sophomore, shared, "During the unit on the Constitution, when we got to the First Amendment, my teacher said, 'This is why we can't let certain ideologies take root here.' Everyone looked at me." Rabia reported, "I wrote my final paper on civil liberties violations post-9/11. My teacher gave me a C+ and wrote 'Try to be more objective' in red ink. The kid who wrote about how great the Patriot Act was got an A."

The parents did something unprecedented: they demanded a public forum. Not a private meeting with administrators. Not a closed-door discussion. A public forum where the community could hear what was happening to Muslim students in government classes that were supposed to teach democratic participation. Principal Smith's first instinct was to refuse. This felt dangerous, potentially inflammatory. But parent organizer Dr. Layla Hassan made it clear, "Our children are being taught that their political voices don't matter. If you won't let us address this publicly, you're proving our point."

Instead of parents politely presenting concerns while administrators took notes, Muslim students spoke directly to a packed auditorium about how neutral education had taught them to self-censor. Non-Muslim students who had witnessed this silencing testified about what they'd seen. The school was forced to self-reflect.

 **Think About It!**

Power and Agency:
1. Who drove change in this case study, and why does that matter? Compare this to the previous case studies where schools initiated reform. What different outcomes resulted from community-led versus institution-led approaches?

2. The parents demanded a public forum rather than a private meeting. What would have been lost if they had followed proper channels? How does public accountability function differently than internal processes?

Challenging Neutrality:

1. The students discovered that controversial topics were only controversial when they affected marginalized communities. Test this in your own context: What topics are considered too divisive? Whose comfort determines these boundaries?

Application Challenge:

You discover Muslim students in your school are self-censoring in political discussions and avoiding certain classes. Traditional diversity approaches haven't created meaningful change. Design an approach that:

- Centers student/family agency rather than institutional management
- Creates genuine accountability rather than performative inclusion
- Addresses root causes of political exclusion
- What would success look like? What risks would you need to navigate?

 ## Classroom Strategies and Activities

Strategy 1: Historicizing Muslim Presence in America

A critical first step in addressing systemic oppression is challenging the perception of Muslims as perpetual foreigners by highlighting the long history of Muslim presence in the United States.

Develop curriculum units that explore the historical presence of Muslims in America, beginning with enslaved African Muslims in the colonial era. Resources like Sylviane Diouf's "Servants of Allah: African Muslims Enslaved in the Americas" and the documentary "Prince Among Slaves" provide historical accounts of early Muslim Americans. These resources challenge the perception that Muslim presence in America is a recent phenomenon requiring special accommodation rather than an integral part of American history.

Create classroom exhibits or digital timelines highlighting Muslim contributions to American development across different historical periods. Include profiles of significant figures like Omar Ibn Said (a Muslim scholar enslaved in the Carolinas who wrote an autobiography in Arabic), Muhammad Ali (whose religious and political stances challenged dominant narratives about patriotism), or Fazlur Rahman Khan (the structural engineer who designed iconic American skyscrapers like Chicago's John Hancock Center). These historical connections help students understand that Muslims have helped build American society rather than being recent additions to it.

Analyzing how American understandings of religious freedom have historically included or excluded Muslim practices is also critical. Examine Supreme Court cases, legislative debates, and public controversies surrounding Muslim religious practices to help students understand how religious freedom has been unevenly applied across different faith traditions. This critical analysis helps students recognize how neutral-seeming principles can be applied in discriminatory ways based on which groups hold social and political power.

Project Idea: A Recovering Lost Narratives research project where students investigate the presence and contributions of Muslims in local or regional history can be a creative means of addressing this. Students conduct archival research, oral history interviews, and analysis of historical records to document Muslim presence in their community's development. Introducing students to the Library of Congress digital archive that hosts the Omar Ibn Said Collection with his autobiography and letters in Arabic from the 1830s is a great example. This project challenges the notion of Muslims as outsiders while developing students' historical research skills. The project could culminate in a public presentation where students share their findings with the broader community, contributing to more accurate public understanding of local history.

Strategy 2: Analyzing Security Discourse in Educational Contexts
The post-9/11 security framework has profoundly shaped educational approaches to Muslim students. More recent policies like the Muslim Ban, expanded ICE operations targeting immigrant communities, and increased surveillance of Muslim student organizations continue this pattern of securitization. These contemporary measures create climates of fear where Muslim students may self-censor their religious and cultural expressions, worry about family separations through deportation, or face added scrutiny.

Guide students in examining how terrorism is framed in educational and media contexts and its impact on educational policies and practices. Analyze patterns in how certain acts of violence are labeled as terrorism (and associated with entire religious communities) while others are framed as isolated incidents committed by "troubled individuals." This analysis helps students recognize the political nature of security classifications and their disproportionate impact on Muslim communities.

Project Idea: Implement a Security Policy Audit project where students analyze school security policies and practices through a civil rights lens. Students research the development and implementation of security measures, interview various stakeholders about their experiences with these policies, and analyze whether the impacts of security practices are distributed equitably across different student groups. This project develops students' critical policy analysis skills while addressing a specific dimension of systemic oppression affecting Muslim students.

Strategy 3: Addressing Geopolitical Contexts of Muslim Experiences
International conflicts and U.S. foreign policy toward Muslim-majority countries significantly impact Muslim American students' educational experiences. Teach students to recognize

how U.S. policy toward Muslim-majority countries shapes domestic treatment of Muslim Americans. Examine historical and contemporary examples of how international conflicts have triggered domestic suspicion or violence against Muslim communities. This analysis helps students understand that anti-Muslim sentiment is not merely personal prejudice, but also is often mobilized for political purposes.

Provide historical context for contemporary conflicts involving Muslim-majority countries. Ensure that curriculum addresses the complex historical developments—including colonialism, Cold War politics, resource extraction, and indigenous resistance movements—that have shaped current situations. Develop students' abilities to recognize and evaluate multiple perspectives on international issues affecting Muslim communities. Include a range of voices from affected regions rather than relying solely on Western interpretations of events.

Project Idea: Students can examine media coverage of a specific international event through a Media Frame Analysis. Students analyze coverage from multiple sources—U.S. mainstream media, international outlets, and sources from the region itself—identifying differences in framing, language, contextual information, and perspectives included. They create comparative analyses that highlight how media choices shape public understanding of events and affect perceptions of Muslim communities both internationally and domestically.

School-Wide Implementation

Conducting Institutional Archeology

To address systemic oppression, schools must examine how historical patterns and political frameworks have shaped their specific institutional development and current practices.

Commission a school history project that examines how national political developments have influenced local educational approaches to Muslim students and communities. This might include researching how the school responded to events like the Iranian Revolution, the Gulf War, or the September 11 attacks. Did policies change? Were Muslim students or staff affected? How did curriculum evolve in response to these events? This institutional memory helps current stakeholders understand that present challenges that have historical roots specific to the school may point to institutional anti-Muslim bias.

Analyze historical patterns in curriculum representation of Muslims and Islam. Review textbooks, reading lists, and instructional materials used over time to identify persistent patterns of misrepresentation or erasure. This analysis helps identify deeply embedded curricular approaches that need transformation rather than simply adding diverse content to problematic existing frameworks.

Transforming Institutional Discourse

Audit institutional communications—including websites, newsletters, announcements, and promotional materials—to identify how Muslims are represented or erased. Are Muslim students visible in communications about school achievements? Are Muslim cultural and religious observances acknowledged in school calendars and announcements? This audit helps identify patterns of institutional erasure that may be invisible to non-Muslim stakeholders. Being attentive to developing institutional language guidelines that promote accurate and respectful representation of Muslims and Islam is also critical. These guidelines should address common pitfalls like conflating cultural practices with religious requirements, using orientalist terminology, or framing Islam as monolithic. They should provide alternative language that recognizes diversity within Muslim communities and avoids treating Muslims as a homogeneous group defined primarily by religion.

Establish protocols for institutional responses to national or international events affecting Muslim communities. These protocols should guide how schools communicate about these events, support affected students and staff, address potential increases in harassment or discrimination, and facilitate constructive educational conversations. Having established protocols helps prevent reactive approaches that might inadvertently reinforce stereotypes or place burdens on Muslim community members to explain events.

Conclusion

Recognizing the systemic nature of racialized oppression against Muslims situated in specific historical, political, and social contexts provides the foundation for creating more equitable educational environments. This recognition must go beyond general awareness of discrimination to specifically address how Orientalist frameworks, security discourse, and exclusion from political legitimacy have created unique patterns of oppression affecting Muslim students.

The case studies presented demonstrate how schools at different levels can address these specific dimensions of Muslim oppression. Eastview Elementary confronted the historical erasure that positions Muslims as perpetually foreign to American identity despite centuries of presence and contribution. Westfield Middle School challenged how security discourse creates patterns of hypervigilance and suspicion that disproportionately impact Muslim students. Central High School addressed how "neutral" approaches to political education often exclude Muslim perspectives and delegitimize Muslim political expression.

These approaches share a common commitment to addressing root causes of oppression rather than merely managing their symptoms. Rather than focusing exclusively on individual prejudice, they examine how historical narratives, institutional structures, and political frameworks create systemic disadvantages for Muslim students.

This work requires sustained commitment, institutional courage, and ongoing learning. It means confronting deeply embedded patterns in American education that often go unquestioned because they reflect broader societal assumptions about Muslims. It means recognizing that seemingly neutral educational approaches—from historical narratives to security protocols to political discourse norms—can reinforce systemic oppression when they fail to account for how different communities are positioned within structures of power.

As we explore subsequent tenets of MusCrit in following chapters, this foundation will inform our approach to addressing identifiability, gender dynamics, counter-narratives, whiteness as property, and allyship. Each of these dimensions intersects with the historical, political, and social contexts examined here, creating complex challenges requiring multifaceted responses. By developing comprehensive understanding of these systemic patterns, educators can create more just and inclusive educational environments for all students.

Resources for Teachers and School Leaders

Academic and Research Resources

- Beydoun, K. A. (2018). *American Islamophobia: Understanding the roots and rise of fear.* University of California Press.
- Love, E. (2017). *Islamophobia and racism in America.* NYU Press.
- Cainkar, L. A. (2009). *Homeland insecurity: The Arab American and Muslim American experience After 9/11.* Russell Sage Foundation.
- Kundnani, A. (2014). *The Muslims are coming! Islamophobia, extremism, and the domestic war on terror.* Verso Books.

Digital Rights and Surveillance Resources

- CUNY CLEAR (Creating Law Enforcement Accountability & Responsibility): "Mapping Muslims: NYPD Spying and its Impact on American Muslims" report and know-your-rights workshops on digital surveillance [www.cunyclear.org]

- Electronic Frontier Foundation: "Surveillance Self-Defense" guide with specific resources for communities under targeted surveillance [ssd.eff.org]
- Muslim Legal Fund of America: Legal resources for Muslims facing surveillance, watchlisting, and digital monitoring with specific guidance for students [mlfa.org]

Curriculum Resources on Civil Rights and Security

- The Advocates for Human Rights: "Energy of a Nation: Immigrants in America" curriculum with specific modules on post-9/11 policies
- Facing History and Ourselves: "Confronting Islamophobia" teaching resources with specific sections on security policies

Organizations Supporting Civil Rights

- Muslim Advocates: Legal resources and educational materials on civil rights issues affecting Muslim students
- Asian Americans Advancing Justice: Resources specifically addressing the intersection of religious and racial discrimination
- National Association of Muslim Lawyers (NAML): Digital rights resources and referrals to attorneys specializing in surveillance and profiling cases

3

Navigating Visible Religious Identity at School

"Maybe some exchanges might be easier if I wasn't wearing the hijab, like people wouldn't get nervous when they first saw me."—Rania

Introduction

I remember being in college, finding an empty classroom to pray in and keeping the lights turned off so I wouldn't get caught praying. There was no designated space on campus to pray. I remember walking to our town's spirit parade, when someone passing by rolled down their window to yell at me to go back home. I remember one of my students with a last name Akbar, sharing the most dreaded part of her day was when attendance was taken in her high school, and the teacher would call her name only to be followed by her classmates jeering "Allahu Akbar" or terrorist.

Identifiability stands at the core of the Muslim American experience, functioning as both an expression of faith and a catalyst for discrimination. For Muslim Americans, the choice to be visibly Muslim carries profound implications that shape every interaction, from casual conversations to educational opportunities. Unlike aspects of identity that can remain private, visible Muslim identity—through a hijab, kufi, beard, or other religious markers—immediately announces one's religious affiliation in every setting.

Muslims navigate this visibility daily when they pray in public spaces, an act required five times daily. Finding appropriate places to pray on campus, adjusting class schedules around prayer times, and managing others' reactions to these practices are constant realities for Muslim youth committed to their faith obligations. These visible markers create situations where Muslim students must navigate others' preconceived notions before they ever speak a word.

This hypervisibility produces what W.E.B. Du Bois called "double consciousness," where individuals experience their identity as divided—seeing themselves simultaneously through their own eyes and through the often-hostile gaze of others. For Muslim Americans, this means experiencing the tension between their American and Muslim identities while perpetually viewing themselves through the eyes of a society that often portrays these identities as incompatible.

Recent research confirms the significance of this visibility and its impact. The CAIR-MA 2025 bullying report found that among female respondents who wear the hijab, 35% experienced physical harassment at school, including incidents of having their hijabs pulled or removed (CAIR-MA, 2025). Similarly, CAIR-California's 2024 Campus Climate Report revealed that over half of Muslim college students (53%) felt targeted by peers because of their religious identity, with particularly high rates (88%) at some institutions. This statistic gained tragic specificity in March 2025 when two 13-year-old Muslim girls at Wallace Middle School in Connecticut were attacked—one punched in the face resulting in a black eye, the other emerging with a cut across her neck.

These challenges have intensified in the current political climate, where identifiable Muslim students report being labeled as extremists or terrorist sympathizers for expressing political views on international issues. Many face surveillance of their social media activities by university administrations or external organizations that compile information on politically active Muslim students, creating a chilling effect on their campus participation. The blacklisting of students through websites that target Muslim activists has created an environment where many identifiable Muslim students self-censor to protect their future employment prospects.

The hypervisibility of being Muslim creates a paradoxical experience—simultaneous prominence and erasure. Muslim students become hypervisible in educational spaces, their religious identity overshadowing all other aspects of their personhood. Yet simultaneously, their complex, multifaceted experiences disappear beneath stereotypical assumptions about what it means to be Muslim. Within this paradox, Muslim students struggle to find spaces where they can simply be themselves without constant explanation or justification.

The decision to be identifiably Muslim therefore represents both an act of faith and, in the current sociopolitical climate, an act of courage and resistance. One student shared, "I'm so ready to represent the Muslim ummah as so many others I know have done before me." This sentiment captures how religious identifiers often hold deep personal meaning for Muslim students, yet these same identifiers also expose them to discrimination ranging from microaggressions to outright harassment. The CAIR-MA report reveals that nearly one-quarter (23%) of Muslim students have "altered or considered altering their appearance, behavior, or name to hide the fact that they are Muslim," demonstrating the heavy burden that identifiability places on Muslim youth.

For educators committed to creating inclusive learning environments, understanding identifiability's impact requires moving beyond general approaches to religious diversity. It demands recognition of the particular challenges that visible Muslim identity creates in educational settings, especially in our current moment of heightened political polarization. This chapter explores how educators can develop classroom practices that support identifiable Muslim students' full participation and belonging, creating spaces where visible faith is respected rather than targeted.

Framing our Conversation

Muslim identifiability isn't just about personal religious expression—it's about how society transforms religious symbols into racial markers. When a Muslim student wears a hijab or grows a beard, these personal acts of faith become public identifiers that trigger a cascade of assumptions. Racialization impacts minoritized populations who are perceived as different and in most cases inferior because of their differences from the mainstream. These visual cues in a racialized experience trigger social categorization and, often, discrimination, and outright demonization and oppression.

Du Bois' (1903) concept of double consciousness perfectly captures what identifiable Muslim students experience daily. They see themselves through their own eyes and simultaneously through America's often suspicious gaze. While Muslim American students may pride themselves in their hyphenated identities, they constantly encounter messaging that treats these identities as contradictory. In classroom discussions about international events, they feel the weight of representing Islam while navigating assumptions about their allegiances. For identifiable Muslim students, their social location is significantly influenced by the visibility of their religious identity, which often places them in a marginalized position within educational settings. This experience is further complicated by intersections with other aspects of identity such as race, gender, class, and immigration status.

For many Muslim Americans, visible religious markers create what Goffman (1963) would call a discredited stigma in contexts where Islam is viewed negatively. This reality confronts Muslim students with complex decisions about identity management—whether to emphasize, downplay, or occasionally conceal their religious identity. The CAIR-MA finding, that nearly a quarter of Muslim students have considered altering their appearance to hide their Muslim identity, reveals how burdensome these calculations become. These dynamics directly impact learning. When students worry about confirming negative stereotypes, they divert mental energy from academics to impression management. This cognitive burden creates unequal educational experiences that educators must recognize and address.

Reflective Practice

When we examine our assumptions about visible religious expression, we often discover internalized narratives that position visible Muslim identity as somehow foreign or potentially concerning. These unconscious biases can affect even well-intentioned educators, shaping how we respond to Muslim students' religious expressions in subtle yet significant ways and in many ways our personal experiences with religious identity inevitably color how we perceive Muslim students' visible faith expressions. Educators from majority religious backgrounds may have limited experience with the hypervisibility that identifiable Muslim students navigate daily. Those from secular backgrounds might struggle to understand why students would choose to wear visible religious markers that could expose them to discrimination. Acknowledging these perspectives helps us recognize potential blind spots in our approach.

Looking closely at classroom interactions often reveals patterns that differentially impact identifiable Muslim students. How often do we call on students with visible religious identifiers compared to their peers? Do we unconsciously assign them roles as cultural representatives rather than seeing their individual strengths? Are identifiable Muslim students participating equally in class discussions, especially when topics touch on international affairs or religious themes?

The curriculum materials we select send powerful messages about whose experiences matter. How do our teaching resources represent visibly Muslim individuals? Are they portrayed only in religious contexts, or are they shown in diverse roles and situations? Do our examples and scenarios acknowledge visible aspects of Muslim identity as normal variations of human experience rather than as exotic or problematic? Materials that naturally include diverse representations help normalize religious diversity for all students.

In today's heightened political climate, consider how rapidly changing geopolitical events impact identifiable Muslim students who often face impossible expectations. Many report being expected to either remain silent on issues affecting their communities or serve as "spokespeople" explaining complex situations they may have no personal connection to beyond their religious identity. Others describe being scrutinized for political expressions that would be considered normal civic engagement from non-Muslim peers. How might these dynamics affect classroom participation and student well-being?

When incidents targeting identifiable Muslim students occur, our responses communicate powerful messages about belonging. Do we address both immediate safety concerns and underlying patterns that enable such targeting? Do we inadvertently minimize religious-based harassment by treating it as less serious than other forms of discrimination? Do we acknowledge the unique vulnerability created by visible religious identifiers that cannot be easily concealed?

Putting it into Action

Elementary: The Books Started It All—Ms. Rivera's 3rd Grade Journey

Carmen Rivera didn't set out to transform how her school approached Muslim identifiability. She just wanted better books.

"I was honestly embarrassed," she admits. "Here I was teaching in a diverse district, and my classroom library had nothing showing kids in hijab or kufi. Nothing showing Muslim families just being families. So, I ordered some books. That's all it was at first."

Those books catalyzed conversations Carmen hadn't anticipated. When Fatima, a quiet Muslim student, saw *Hana's Hundreds of Hijabs* on the shelf, her entire demeanor changed. "She just lit up and carried it around for days," Carmen recalls. "Then other kids got curious. Not in a bad way—just kids being kids."

Rather than delivering a formal lesson on Islam, Carmen simply answered questions as they emerged. When Jason asked why the character wore "that thing on her head," Carmen kept it straightforward, "It's called hijab. Some Muslim women wear it as part of their faith, like how some people wear cross necklaces."

The classroom culture shifted subtly. Carmen noticed Fatima participating more frequently in discussions. Muslim and non-Muslim students began incorporating diverse religious identifiers in their creative writing and artwork without prompting. During community circle, conversations about identity emerged organically.

"The most powerful moment came during parent-teacher conferences," Carmen reflects. "Fatima's mother told me, tears in her eyes, that her daughter had started proudly wearing her hijab to soccer practice. Before, she'd always pull it off the minute school ended."

Not everything went smoothly. When a substitute teacher asked Fatima to remove her "hat" in class, students immediately corrected him with "That's not a hat. That's hijab." Carmen used this moment to help her class discuss how they could respect each other's identities even when adults made mistakes.

For their community helpers project, Carmen invited professionals from diverse backgrounds, including visibly Muslim community members. "I didn't make a big deal about it," she says. "They just came in as the pediatrician, the engineer, the police officer who happened to wear hijab or have a beard."

By year's end, the transformation was remarkable. During the school art show, Carmen overheard a parent asking her daughter about a drawing that included a girl in hijab. The child shrugged, "That's just how Sophia looks. Like I have curly hair and Tim has glasses."

"That's when I knew something important had happened," Carmen says. "For these kids, visible Muslim identity had become just another normal human variation. No big deal. Just part of who their friends are."

Middle School: They're Watching Us, Right?—Identity Navigation in Mr. Hall's Classroom

September 4th—First day of school
James Hall watches Ahmed enter his 7th-grade social studies classroom, carefully scanning for the best seat. Ahmed chooses a desk against the wall, partially hidden by a bookshelf. James makes a mental note.

September 18th—After class
"Mr. Hall? Can I ask you something?" Ahmed lingers after the bell.

"Sure, what's up?"

"Do you think it's weird that I pray during lunch?" Ahmed's question comes in a rush. "Some kids were saying it's weird, and one kid asked if I was, you know... being radical or something."

James takes a breath. This isn't in any teaching manual.

"Ahmed, prayer isn't weird. Different people pray in different ways. Some quietly, some visibly. But we should talk about that 'radical' comment because that's not okay."

October 3rd—Team meeting
"I'm noticing something concerning," James tells his colleagues. "Our Muslim students with visible religious practices—Ahmed with his kufi, Noor and Samira with their hijabs—they're self-isolating. They're choosing seats away from other students, not participating in discussions about current events, even though they were engaged last year."

"What do you suggest?" asks the team leader. "We could host a diversity assembly?"

James shakes his head. "I think we need something more organic. I have an idea for my classroom that might help."

October 15th—Classroom
"Today we're starting a new approach to our identity unit," James announces. "Instead of me teaching, you'll be the researchers exploring how people navigate identity across cultures."

The project engages students immediately. Working in diverse groups, they investigate questions like "How do people show important parts of their identity?" and "When do people highlight or downplay aspects of who they are?"

Ahmed's group researches how athletes express religious identity in sports. They discover Muslim football players who pray after touchdowns, Jewish baseball players who won't play on holy days, and Christian athletes who point skyward after scoring.

"So it's not just Muslims who show their religion?" Ahmed asks during his group's planning session.

"Nope," replies his teammate Zoe. "My uncle wears a cross necklace all the time. Isn't it sort of the same thing."

November 8th—Classroom discussion

The conversation turns to Malcolm X after students read excerpts from his autobiography.

"I never knew he was Muslim," says Jason. "We always just learn about him as a Black leader."

"His Muslim identity was central to his later activism," James explains. "Notice how his understanding of Islam transformed after his hajj pilgrimage."

After class, Samira approaches James. "That was the first time anyone's talked about Malcolm X being Muslim. Usually, teachers just skip that part."

December 12th—Hallway conversation

James overhears a conversation between Ahmed and another student:

"Is that for your religion?" the student asks, pointing to Ahmed's kufi.

"Yeah, it's called a kufi. Some Muslim guys wear them, especially for prayer. Not everyone though—it's a personal choice."

"Cool. Is it like a requirement or something?"

"Not exactly. It's more of a way to show respect. Kind of like how some people take off their hats in church."

The conversation continues normally. No awkwardness, no defensive posturing. Just kids talking.

May 15th—End of year reflection
"What surprised me most," James writes in his teaching journal, "was how addressing identifiability required no special curriculum. It needed thoughtful integration into existing content, creating space for student agency, and modeling matter-of-fact engagement with religious identity. The biggest change wasn't in what I taught, but in how I approached the visible aspects of religious identity—as normal human variation rather than as problems to be managed."

High School: Literature as Liberation—An English Teacher Confronts Surveillance Culture

The email marked "URGENT" arrived at 10:37 PM.

"Ms. Johnson, please don't use my real name when posting grades for the Muslim-American literature essay. There are websites tracking Muslim students who write about political topics. I'm worried about getting blacklisted for college."

Angela Johnson stared at her screen, her stomach tightening. Fatima, one of her most promising AP English students, had chosen to analyze Mohja Kahf's poetry about hijab for their American Voices assignment. Nothing in her essay was remotely political—it was a literary analysis of symbolism and metaphor. Yet here was Fatima, afraid of being monitored for simply engaging with literature that reflected her identity.

This wasn't the first time Angela had encountered the chilling effect of surveillance on her identifiable Muslim students. Last semester, Omar had declined to participate in a recorded class discussion about post-9/11 literature. Amina had asked to submit a written reflection instead of joining the class debate about religious symbolism in public spaces.

Angela hadn't planned to become an advocate for Muslim students navigating hypervisibility. She'd simply wanted to create an AP English curriculum that actually reflected American literary diversity. After noticing that her syllabus included Jewish, Christian, Buddhist and secular voices but no Muslim American authors, she'd integrated works by G. Willow Wilson, Reem Faruqi, and Mohja Kahf alongside established canon.

"These aren't 'diverse additions,'" she told her department when presenting the revised curriculum. "These are essential American voices that have been excluded from our literary conversation. Our Muslim students deserve to see themselves in AP curriculum, and all students benefit from engaging with the full spectrum of American literary experience."

The texts created natural openings for discussions of identifiability. When they read Kahf's "Hijab Scene #7," students encountered lines "No, I'm not bald under the scarf/No, I'm not from that countrywhere women can't drive cars" which sparked organic conversations about hypervisibility, assumptions, and the complexity of religious expression.

Angela paired contemporary Muslim American texts with classics addressing similar themes. Reading Du Bois's exploration of double consciousness alongside Wilson's memoir about converting to Islam created powerful connections across different historical contexts. Students recognized parallel patterns while identifying the unique dimensions of religious identifiability. The current political climate created additional considerations that Angela hadn't initially anticipated. After campus protests about international conflicts led to Muslim students being surveilled, Angela noticed her visibly Muslim students becoming more guarded in classroom discussions.

Her response was practical rather than political. She created alternative assessment options, allowing students to choose between class discussions, written reflections, or small group conversations. She established clear communication about which classroom activities might be recorded or shared. Most importantly, she consulted directly with affected students about what would help them engage authentically while protecting their wellbeing.

"I'm not teaching politics," Angela explained when a parent questioned her curriculum choices. "I'm teaching American literature—all of it. That includes Muslim American experiences, just as it includes the experiences of other religious and cultural groups that have contributed to our literary tradition."

Angela's classroom demonstrated how thoughtfully selected literature could create space for exploring religious identifiability without exceptionalizing or tokenizing Muslim students. Through storytelling, students encountered the complexity of visible Muslim identity while developing greater awareness of how identifiability shapes human experience across different contexts.

Think About It!

Questions for Reflective Analysis:

1. How did each teacher integrate attention to Muslim identifiability within existing curriculum rather than treating it as an add-on?
2. What approaches helped normalize visible Muslim identity without exceptionalizing Muslim students?
3. How did these teachers balance acknowledging the reality of discrimination while avoiding portraying Muslim students as victims?
4. What role did student agency play in each classroom approach?
5. Which specific strategies might you adapt for your own classroom context?

Classroom Strategies and Activities

Strategy 1: Normalizing Visible Muslim Identity in Classroom Culture

Rather than treating Muslim identifiability as something requiring special accommodation, effective educators weave visible Muslim identity into the fabric of classroom life. This normalization begins with the visual environment itself. The images on your walls, the books on your shelves, and the examples in your presentations should naturally include visibly Muslim individuals in diverse contexts—not just religious settings, but as scientists, artists, athletes, and historical figures. When students see identifiable Muslims represented across domains, their presence becomes expected rather than exceptional.

Language patterns powerfully shape perceptions of what's "normal." Examine how you discuss religious practices and symbols in your classroom. Do you frame Islamic practices as exotic or foreign? Do you use "we" and "they" language that positions identifiable Muslims outside the classroom community? Small shifts in language can transform religious identifiers from markers of difference to expressions of cultural diversity.

The way you structure classroom routines sends powerful messages about whose needs matter. Consider how your regular procedures might unintentionally disadvantage Muslim students with visible identifiers. During Ramadhan, could morning activities be less physically demanding? Could class celebrations incorporate halal options without making Muslim students request them? These thoughtful adjustments communicate that Muslim identifiability belongs in the classroom rather than requiring special exceptions.

When students notice or ask about visible religious differences, your response sets the tone for how these differences will be perceived. Teachers can often model respectful inquiry saying something like "That's a great observation. In our classroom, people express their identities in many ways. Some people wear hijab as part of their Muslim faith, just like others might wear cross necklaces or yarmulkes."

Project Idea: Identity Expression Gallery. Students investigate how people express important aspects of their identity through visible markers across cultures and religions. Each student can research one form of identity expression (religious attire, cultural clothing, body art, etc.) by interviewing community members, researching historical contexts, and examining contemporary practices. Their findings are presented through creative displays combining images, quotes, and contextual information. The gallery installation remains in the classroom as a visual reminder of the diversity of identity expressions, with Muslim identifiability presented as one natural part of this human diversity rather than as something exotic or concerning.

Strategy 2: Building Student Agency Around Identity Expression

Identity development involves navigating complex choices about self-expression, particularly for students from marginalized groups. Rather than prescribing how Muslim students should navigate identifiability, effective educators create opportunities for all students to explore identity expression as a universal human experience. Student-led inquiry projects allow them to examine questions of identity expression on their own terms. When a middle school teacher noticed tensions arising around a student who had recently begun wearing hijab, she introduced a broader exploration of how people express important aspects of identity. Students investigated questions like: "How do people show what matters to them through clothing?" "How do others respond to visible markers of identity?" and "How do people decide when to highlight or downplay aspects of identity?" This approach positioned Muslim identifiability within a universal framework of identity navigation rather than as an isolated phenomenon to be grappled with. The intersection of identifiability and institutional discrimination appears starkly in athlete Bilqis Abdul-Qaadir's experience. Despite scoring 3,070 points in her Massachusetts high school career, setting the all-time state record, FIBA's hijab ban ended her professional basketball dreams. She had played 100s of high school and college games and her hijab never harmed her or any of her opponents. Only after years of advocacy did FIBA reverse the policy in 2017.

Classroom dialogues about code-switching and contextual identity expression help students recognize that everyone modulates self-presentation in different contexts. Discussions might explore questions like: "How do you express yourself differently at school versus at home?" "What aspects of your identity do you highlight in different situations?" and "How do you decide when to emphasize certain parts of who you are?"

Project Idea: "Identity Journeys Digital Storytelling" Students create digital narratives documenting their own or others' experiences with identity expression, addressing questions like: "How has my relationship with expressing my identity changed over time?" "What factors influence how

I express important aspects of who I am?" and "How do others' responses affect my identity choices?" For Muslim students, this might include exploring their journey with hijab, beard, or other religious identifiers. For non-Muslim students, it might involve other aspects of identity expression. The project can culminate in a classroom showcase where students share stories and identify common themes in identity navigation.

Strategy 3: Addressing Intersectional Dimensions of Muslim Identifiability

Muslim identifiability never exists in isolation—it always intersects with other aspects of identity to create unique educational experiences. Gender dramatically shapes how Muslim identifiability is perceived and experienced. Girls report more physical harassment related to religious attire, while boys more often face security-related suspicion. Class discussions might examine how gender norms influence reactions to religious expression and how Muslim women exercise agency through diverse approaches to modesty.

Race and ethnicity create another critical intersection with Muslim identifiability. Black Muslims, Arab Muslims, South Asian Muslims, and white Muslims each navigate different terrain when their religious identity becomes visible. A Black Muslim student wearing hijab encounters different assumptions than an Arab Muslim in the same attire. Classroom activities might explore how media representations reinforce certain racial-religious stereotypes while leaving other Muslim identities invisible. I recall a funny incident when a local public-school teacher reached out to me to help speak with some girls in his class who had recently arrived as refugees from another country. While this is akin to the black male teacher being asked to speak with the black male students when they get in trouble, I obliged and went to meet the 4th to 6th grade girls. The teacher was being gracious, but in the absence of religious information and support, the girls were giving him a run for it. They would go hang out in the bathroom, making a huge mess, under the pretext that they needed to make ablution for the afternoon prayer. I didn't speak their language, but the moment they saw someone that looked like them, and managed to convey to them that making ablution doesn't take that long or require creating puddles they giggled apologetically. There are many things to consider here—the inadequate knowledge base of educators regarding diverse student backgrounds, the lack of representation, diverse recruitment and hiring, but also what it meant for these students to see someone else who was just as identifiable as them.

Immigration status adds another layer of complexity to Muslim identifiability. Students who are immigrants or refugees often navigate not only religious visibility but also linguistic and cultural differences. The current political climate has created heightened vulnerability for Muslim students with uncertain immigration status or family members affected by travel restrictions. Recent security measures targeting students from Muslim-majority countries have created additional stressors for many identifiable Muslim students.

In today's polarized environment, political tensions have created new dimensions of vulnerability for identifiable Muslim students. Following campus protests over conflicts in Gaza and other regions, Muslim students with visible religious identifiers report facing assumptions about their political views based solely on their appearance. Some describe being monitored by campus security during peaceful protests or having their social media accounts scrutinized by university administrations. Others fear being added to blacklisting websites that could jeopardize future employment. These contemporary realities add new layers to the challenges of Muslim identifiability.

Project Idea: "Intersectional Identity Maps" Students analyze how different aspects of identity interact to shape lived experiences in educational contexts. Using identity mapping techniques, they explore questions like: "How do different aspects of identity become more or less salient in various settings?" "How do multiple aspects of identity create unique challenges or opportunities?" and "How do people navigate complex, intersecting identities in different contexts?" For Muslim students, this might involve examining how religious identifiability intersects with gender, race, class, and other factors. The project emphasizes the diversity within Muslim identifiability rather than treating it as a monolithic experience. Students create visual representations of these intersections and discuss implications for creating more inclusive learning environments.

School-Wide Implementation

All educators are school leaders in some particular way. While you may think school-wide implementation is like low-hanging fruit, how to implement may not be obvious. The section below provides ideas that can also be practiced in the classroom and advocated for with school leadership.

Creating a Culture of Religious Respect and Accommodation

Effective support for identifiable Muslim students requires coordinated effort across the entire school community. Begin with policy development that explicitly addresses religious expression and accommodation. Clearly affirm students' right to religious expression, including wearing religious attire, observing religious holidays, and participating in practices like daily prayer or fasting in Ramadhan. Streamline accommodation procedures rather than requiring Muslim students to make special requests that highlight their difference.

The CAIR-MA report found that 65% of Muslim students reported that their schools failed to issue statements, provide accommodations, or address significant issues impacting the Muslim community, such as Ramadhan or Eid. Design physical spaces to communicate inclusion of religious diversity through both functional accommodations and symbolic representations. Creating multifaith reflection rooms that serve diverse student needs or specific Muslim prayer rooms is essential. Include images and information that normalize religious diversity, including visible Muslim identity, as part of the school community. Providing a space for Muslim students to change with additional privacy than most standard locker rooms and allowing for modest athletic attire is another critical piece. Provide clear information about meal ingredients to respect religious dietary restrictions without requiring students to make special inquiries. Food laws pertaining to Muslim students include food choices that are halal or kosher.

Visual Representation
The visual landscape of school buildings sends powerful messages about whose identities belong. Thoughtful inclusion of identifiable Muslims in hallway displays, library collections, and digital communications normalizes visible religious identity. This visual inclusion extends classroom representation efforts into common areas where identity messages reach the entire school community. Specific approaches include ensuring school promotional materials naturally include identifiable Muslim students, featuring diverse religious identities in career and college readiness materials, displaying student artwork that explores identity expression across cultures, and creating library displays that include books featuring visibly Muslim characters.

Conclusion

Addressing the pivotal role of identifiability in Muslim students' experiences transforms educational environments from spaces where visible religious difference is marginalized to communities where religious diversity is recognized as valuable. This work requires moving beyond superficial approaches to developing substantive understanding of how identifiability shapes Muslim students' daily experiences and identity formation. By implementing approaches shared in this chapter, educators can help create educational environments where identifiable Muslim students experience true belonging rather than perpetual othering. In these environments, Muslim students can navigate their double consciousness not as a burden but as a resource, drawing on the insights that come from inhabiting multiple identity positions to make unique contributions to their educational communities.

Resources for Teachers and School Leaders

Identity Development and Expression Resources

- Sirin, S. R., & Fine, M. (2008). *Muslim American youth: Understanding hyphenated identities through multiple methods*. New York University Press.
- Peek, L. (2017). *Behind the backlash: Muslim Americans after 9/11*. Temple University Press.
- Yaqeen Institute for Islamic Research: [yaqeeninstitute.org]
- Zaal, M. (2012). Islamophobia in classrooms, media, and politics. *Journal of Adolescent & Adult Literacy*, 55(6), 555–558.

Classroom Resources for Supporting Religious Identity

- Islamic Networks Group (ING): "Religious Practices of Muslim Students in Public Schools"—Comprehensive guide addressing practical accommodations for prayer, Ramadhan, and other visible aspects of Muslim faith in educational settings [ing.org]
- Teaching While Muslim: [teachingwhilemuslim.org]

Literature Featuring Identifiable Muslim Characters

- Faruqi, R. (2015). *Lailah's lunchbox: A Ramadan story*. Tilbury House Publishers. Picture book about a Muslim girl navigating Ramadan at school.
- Abdel-Fattah, R. (2005). *Does my head look big in this?*. Pan Macmillan. Young adult novel about a Muslim Australian girl choosing to wear hijab.

- Wilson, G. W. (2014–2019). *Ms. Marvel* comic series. Marvel Comics. Award-winning series featuring Kamala Khan, a visibly Muslim superhero.

Classroom Management Resources for Identity-Based Incidents

- Tanenbaum Center for Interreligious Understanding: [tanenbaum.org]

4

Understanding Gender and Faith in Student Experiences

"I feel they have common misconceptions with that and, honestly, I don't really blame them because, if I were to view Islam the way that society and social media portrays it, I would have the same view. I think it just takes people who are willing to actually explain the way that religion is practiced and what it actually represents."—Sana

Introduction

We were taking a break at a rest area while driving from New Jersey to Massachusetts. At that point in my life, I used to wear the niqab (face-covering) as an expression of my faith. I sat at a table while the rest of my family went to grab coffee. One man clearly disturbed and worried by my visual existence spoke to his friend in a way that was clearly distressed and heartbroken at my assumed subjugation. Also, assuming I was not from here, and didn't speak English, he spoke to his friend about the unfairness of it all, of how my husband could force me to look this way, or had my husband ever considered if he would treat his own daughter this way?

I am as mortified by this incident now as I was then.

I did nothing in that moment.

I was too distressed to act in that moment, to dismantle stereotypes or anything of the sort. When you are the recipient of bigotry, whether it is hostile or seeping in the waters of white saviorism, there are many things that happen all at once—there is a conflicting emotional and intellectual overload; you consider the profile of the oppressor, the public space you are in, the people around you, your own children and whether they have overheard this or not, you decide whether you want to make a "big deal" of a (not) microaggression or not, you wonder if you are feeling grounded enough to take this forward, or if you are too enraged, upset, sad; you wonder if it's worth it, and you ask do I carry the burden of correcting them because this is about me and us, or do I let go? All this in a compressed byte of time. So, yes, in that moment, I said nothing; I pretended like I hadn't heard or understood. My little boys hadn't heard it; my husband had not either. Later when I shared with my husband what had happened he was equally surprised that I said nothing.

In the above quote Sana is explaining how she had to educate her teacher about misconceptions regarding women in Islam, including the false belief that Muslim women "weren't allowed to drive cars" and correcting these stereotypes by explaining the difference between cultural practices and Islamic teachings. Gender plays a pivotal role in how Muslim American students experience educational spaces. The intersection of gender with Muslim identity creates unique challenges and opportunities that educators must recognize to create truly inclusive learning environments. The mainstream narrative about Muslim women often oscillates between portraying them as oppressed victims in need of rescue or as exotic others, while Muslim men are frequently depicted as controlling or threatening. These gendered stereotypes infiltrate educational spaces, shaping interactions, expectations, and opportunities for Muslim students.

The hypervisibility of Muslim women who wear hijab creates a particular experience of scrutiny and stereotyping that impacts their educational journeys. The decision to wear hijab makes religious identity immediately visible, resulting in assumptions about capabilities, beliefs, and freedom of choice. There is also a reverse scenario that often occurs where the identifiable female Muslim student's gaze is avoided, and she is skipped over as if she is invisible.

Muslim male students face different but equally challenging stereotypes, particularly around assumptions of aggression, religious extremism, and attitudes toward women. These assumptions can shape interactions with peers and teachers, affecting everything from group work assignments to disciplinary actions. The racialization of Muslim male identity—particularly for those who are visibly Muslim due to names, beards, or other signifiers—creates vulnerabilities that impact their educational experiences.

Both groups experience profound invisibility, though in gender-specific ways. The academic strengths, leadership potential, and individual personalities of Muslim students are often rendered invisible beneath assumptions about their religious identity. In classroom discussions about gender equality, Muslim girls frequently find themselves in an impossible position—either hypervisible as they're called upon to explain or defend their religious practices or invisible as their perspectives on feminism and empowerment are dismissed.

On October 14, 2023, six-year-old Wadea Al-Fayoume ran toward his family's landlord for a hug. Instead, Joseph Czuba stabbed the Palestinian-American boy 26 times, telling the child's mother, "you Muslims must die" (Chicago Sun-Times, 2023). Wadea's murder in Plainfield Township, Illinois, represents the lethal endpoint of gendered racialization, where even young Muslim boys are perceived as future threats requiring elimination. This gendered paradox intensifies during adolescence when identity formation intersects with increasing awareness of others' perceptions. Muslim boys may engage in self-censorship to appear less threatening, while Muslim girls navigate complex tensions between expressing their religious identity and avoiding unwanted attention or stereotyping. These daily negotiations require significant emotional labor that can detract from their educational experience and sense of belonging in school communities (Buchanan & Settles, 2019).

Educators can address this paradox by cultivating classroom environments that recognize the gendered dimensions of Muslim students' experiences without reinforcing stereotypes. This includes avoiding assumptions about Muslim girls' agency or Muslim boys' attitudes, creating space for diverse expressions of Muslim masculinity and femininity, and ensuring curriculum materials represent Muslim men and women in nuanced, contemporary contexts rather than through orientalist stereotypes.

This chapter explores the intersection of gender and Muslim identity in educational contexts, providing strategies for creating learning environments that acknowledge and address these complex dynamics.

Framing our Conversation

The intersection of gender, religion, and ethnicity creates complex realities for Muslim American students. Drawing on intersectionality theory, first articulated by Kimberlé Crenshaw, we can understand how multiple aspects of identity interact to create unique experiences of privilege and marginalization. For Muslim American students, gender identity intersects with religious identity, racial identity, socioeconomic status, immigration status, and other factors to shape their educational experiences in particular ways. Gender plays a crucial role in the racialization process that affects Muslim Americans. The visible markers of Muslim religious identity particularly the hijab for women create gendered experiences of surveillance, questioning, and stereotyping. The gendered nature of anti-Muslim violence extends across age groups. Three Palestinian students shot in Burlington, Vermont, on November 25, 2023, Hisham Awartani, Kinnan Abdalhamid, and Tahseen Ali Ahmad were targeted while wearing keffiyehs and speaking Arabic. Awartani remains paralyzed from the chest down after the bullet struck his spinal cord. Meanwhile, in Warner Robbins, Georgia, teacher Benjamin Reese was arrested for threatening to "slit [a Muslim student's] throat" and "cut her head off."

Critical feminist theories provide additional insights into how gender expectations shape Muslim students' educational experiences. These theories highlight how dominant cultural narratives about appropriate gender roles and expressions can marginalize individuals whose practices differ from mainstream norms. For Muslim students, this might manifest in assumptions about gender segregation, participation in certain activities, or career aspirations. These assumptions can come from both within and outside Muslim communities, creating complex challenges of navigation. Islamic feminist scholarship has challenged the false binary that positions Islam as inherently oppressive to women. It documents how young Muslim women and men often find empowerment through, rather than despite, their religious identities, drawing on Islamic concepts of justice and equity to advocate for gender equality in ways that respect their faith commitments. This scholarship provides crucial resources for educators seeking to move beyond stereotypical representations of Muslim gender dynamics.

When educational environments address the complexities of Muslim identity, including its gendered aspects, Muslim students report greater sense of belonging, academic engagement, and psychological well-being. Conversely, environments that ignore or stereotype these experiences contribute to feelings of alienation and academic disengagement.

Reflective Practice

Gender shapes every aspect of our work as educators, often in ways we don't recognize until we pause to examine our practices through this lens. For those of us working with Muslim students, this reflection becomes even more essential because mainstream narratives about Muslim gender experiences are so thoroughly saturated with stereotypes and misconceptions. Most of us have absorbed these narratives through years of media exposure, political discourse, and even well-intentioned multicultural education that sometimes reduces complex religious traditions to simplified cultural practices. We carry these internalized images into our classrooms—Muslim girls portrayed as lacking agency, Muslim boys as potentially controlling or aggressive—without realizing how they influence our interactions, expectations, and decisions.

These assumptions surface in subtle ways: the surprise we feel when a hijabi student excels in STEM subjects; the unconscious monitoring of Muslim boys' interactions with female classmates; the lowered expectations for Muslim girls' career aspirations; the discomfort with traditional gender expressions that differ from secular Western norms. Our curriculum choices often reveal these unconscious biases. Look across your teaching materials—do Muslim women appear primarily as objects of religious restriction rather than as scientists, artists, athletes, and leaders? Are Muslim men shown only in contexts of religious authority or political conflict rather than as caregivers, collaborators, and creators? These representational patterns send powerful messages about possibilities and limitations.

Our classroom interactions similarly reflect gendered assumptions. Do we call on Muslim students differently based on gender? Do we assign different types of leadership roles? Do we respond differently to assertive behavior from Muslim boys versus girls? These patterns create different educational experiences for students across gender expressions. Even our well-intentioned efforts to promote gender equity sometimes reflect limited understanding of diverse religious perspectives. We might inadvertently position Western secular frameworks as inherently "progressive" while viewing religious approaches to gender as automatically "traditional" or "restrictive"—a false binary that erases the complex feminist traditions within Islam and the agency of Muslim women and men in interpreting their faith traditions.

The path toward more responsive practice begins with noticing—paying attention to these patterns in our teaching materials, classroom interactions, and internal responses. It continues with curiosity—seeking to understand the diverse ways Muslim students and families conceptualize gender rather than imposing our own frameworks.

 **Putting it into Action**

Case Study 1: Elementary School: The Ripple Effect

Snapshot 1: Tuesday, October 3rd, 10:15 AM *Community Helpers Circle Time*

"My mom builds bridges," announces Zara, her hijab slightly askew from morning recess. She's holding the plastic hard hat from the career dress-up bin.

"Girls can't be engineers," interrupts Marcus. "That's for boys."

Twenty-two third-graders turn to look at Zara. Her teacher, Mrs. Tuan, opens her mouth to respond, but Zara beats her to it.

"Yes they can. My mom shows me her blueprints every night. She wears hijab and builds bridges."

"Prove it," challenges Marcus.

"Okay," says Zara simply. "I will."

Snapshot 2: Friday, October 6th, 3:30 PM *After School Pickup*
Zara drags her mother, Dr. Amina Hassan, toward Mrs. Tuan's classroom. "Mama, you have to come show them!"

Dr. Hassan, still in her site safety gear, follows her determined daughter. In her hands: a tablet full of bridge photos and a small model of the suspension bridge project she's managing.

"Mrs. Tuan, this is my mom. She builds bridges. Can she show the class?"

Mrs. Tuan looks at Dr. Hassan's kind eyes, the dirt on her boots, the engineering plans tucked under her arm. "Would you like to visit us Monday?"

Snapshot 3: Monday, October 9th, 9:00 AM *Show and Tell Revolution*
Dr. Hassan doesn't just visit. She brings three colleagues: Maya (hijabi environmental engineer), James (Black male civil engineer), and Sofia (Latina mechanical engineer).

"We all build different things," Dr. Hassan explains, spreading out blueprints. "But we all solve problems."

Hands shoot up around the circle.

"Are there boy nurses?" asks Emma. "Can girls be firefighters?" wonders Aiden. "Do men teach kindergarten?" inquires Sam.

Mrs. Tuan watches as her students' questions multiply faster than she can answer them.

Snapshot 4: Wednesday, October 18th, 11:45 AM *Lunch Investigation Time*
The classroom has transformed into an investigation center. Students cluster around laptops, interview clipboards, and poster boards titled "Jobs Everyone Can Do."

Marcus and Zara work together now, interviewing Mr. Rodriguez, the school's male nurse.

"I wanted to help people feel better," he explains. "That's what nurses do."

Marcus carefully writes: "Nurses help people. Boys and girls can be nurses."

Snapshot 5: Friday, October 27th, 2:00 PM *The Presentation*
Fourth-graders file into Mrs. Tuan's room for the "Job Fair Facts" presentation. Third-graders stand beside poster boards showing doctors, teachers, engineers, firefighters, pilots all represented by diverse faces and genders.

Case Study 2: Middle School: The Perfect Storm
THE PLAYERS:

- Aaliyah, 7th grade: Sent home for "distracting" hijab style
- Ms. Jackson, English teacher: Aaliyah's advocate
- Principal Martinez: Caught between policy and principle
- Mrs. Okafor, Aaliyah's mother: Software engineer, school board candidate
- The Henderson family: Filed the original modest dress complaint
- Student voices: Aaliyah's classmates

DAY 1: THE INCIDENT *Tuesday, March 7th, 8:47 AM*

> **Principal Martinez:** "The assistant principal called me at 8:45. Aaliyah had been sent to the office for dress code violation. Her hijab was 'decorative' rather than 'plain religious covering' according to our policy."

Aaliyah: "It was just a different fabric. Still covered everything the same way. But it had small gold threads woven through it. Mom bought it for my birthday."

Ms. Jackson: "I was teaching when they pulled Aaliyah from my class. To me her hijab looked exactly like what she wears every day. The only difference was it was prettier."

DAY 1: THE EXPLOSION *Tuesday, March 7th, 11:30 AM*

Mrs. Okafor: "I got a call at work saying my daughter was suspended for her hijab being 'too decorative.' I left a client meeting and drove straight to school."

Principal Martinez: "Mrs. Okafor arrived upset. Understandably. But we have policies. The Henderson family complained last month about religious clothing being 'distracting.' The school board directed us to enforce stricter guidelines."

Ms. Jackson: "I could hear raised voices from the main office. Then I saw news vans pulling up. Someone had called the media."

DAY 2: CLASSROOM LABORATORY *Wednesday, March 8th, First Period*

Ms. Jackson: "With Aaliyah suspended, my class was asking questions. I decided to turn it into a learning opportunity rather than avoid the elephant in the room."

Jamal, 7th grader: "Ms. Jackson asked us to research dress codes. Not just ours, but everywhere. She said we were going to become experts."

Emma, 7th grader: "We found out dress codes are really weird. Like, some schools ban yoga pants but allow short shorts. It didn't make sense."

DAY 3: STUDENT MOBILIZATION *Thursday, March 9th, Lunch*

Devin, 7th grader: "We started a petition during lunch. Not just for Aaliyah, but asking the school board to review the whole dress code."

Ms. Jackson: "I didn't organize the petition. The students did that themselves. I just provided them information about how school board meetings work."

Maria, 7th grader: "By Friday, we had 847 signatures. Even kids who didn't know Aaliyah signed it."

DAY 5: COMMUNITY RESPONSE *Sunday, March 12th, Community Center*

Mrs. Okafor: "Parents started reaching out. Not just Muslim families. Families whose daughters were sent home for spaghetti straps, whose sons were disciplined for hair length. We realized this was bigger than Aaliyah's hijab."

Ms. Jackson: "I attended the community meeting as an observer. Watching parents and students strategize together was remarkable."

THE RESOLUTION: SCHOOL BOARD MEETING *Tuesday, March 21st, 7:00 PM*

Principal Martinez: "The school board meeting was packed. Students, parents, teachers, community members. I'd never seen anything like it."

Aaliyah: "I spoke for two minutes. I said my hijab doesn't distract from learning. It helps me feel confident to learn."

Devin: "After Aaliyah spoke, twelve other students spoke. About hair discrimination, about body shaming, about feeling targeted."

Mrs. Henderson: "I realized my complaint about 'distracting' religious clothing had created something I didn't intend. These kids weren't trying to be disruptive. They were just being themselves."

EPILOGUE: ONE MONTH LATER

Principal Martinez: "The new dress code policy is two pages shorter and focuses on safety rather than aesthetics. Aaliyah's back in class, wearing whatever hijab she chooses."

Ms. Jackson: "The students learned more about civic engagement from those two weeks than from any textbook lesson I could have taught."
Aaliyah: "I learned my voice matters. And that standing up for yourself sometimes means standing up for everyone."

Case Study 3: High School: The Masterclass

AP Literature, Period 3 *Ms. Robert's Classroom, Thursday, November 16th*

The observer enters mid-discussion. Seventeen students sit in a loose circle, copies of Mohja Kahf's poetry collection open on their desks. The classroom walls display a mix of classic and contemporary authors—Dickinson beside Darwish, Shakespeare next to Satrapi.

"So when Kahf writes 'I am not your symbol,' who is she addressing?" Ms. Robert asks, not calling on anyone specific.

Hands rise around the circle. She nods to David, a white student near the window.

"Maybe people who want to use Muslim women as examples of oppression? Like, making them represent something they didn't choose to represent?"

"Mm-hmm. Aisha, what do you think?"

Aisha, wearing a burgundy hijab, leans forward. "I think she's talking to everyone who wants her to be either completely oppressed or completely liberated. Like she can't just be... normal."

"Can you say more about 'normal'?"

"Like, in media, Muslim women are either victims who need saving or exceptional women who overcame Islam. But most of us are just regular people with regular problems."

Murmurs of understanding ripple through the circle. The observer notes that several non-Muslim students are nodding thoughtfully.

Ms. Robert doesn't highlight the exchange as special. Instead, she builds on it naturally.

"Let's look at the line 'I'm just a woman in a scarf.' How does this connect to what Aisha just said about being regular people?"

Marcus, an African American student, raises his hand. "It's like how people treat me differently if I wear a hoodie versus a button-down. The clothing becomes bigger than the person."

"That's an interesting parallel, Marcus. Are there other examples in your own lives?"

For the next twenty minutes, students share experiences of being reduced to symbols—the smart Asian student, the athletic Black student, the artistic gay student. Muslim students contribute naturally without being spotlighted.

The observer notices that Ms. Robert manages the discussion expertly, ensuring Muslim voices are included but not burdened with representing all Muslim experiences.

When Sarah, a Somali student, mentions feeling pressure to excel academically "to prove Muslim girls can succeed," several students of different backgrounds express similar pressures they face.

"So we're seeing themes of representation, expectation, and individual agency," Ms. Robert summarizes. "How does Kahf navigate these in her poetry?"

Students return to textual analysis, but the personal connections have deepened their literary understanding.

After Class: The Visiting Teacher's Questions

Ms. Smith, visiting from another district, approaches Ms. Robert as students file out.

"That was incredible. How do you create space for those conversations without tokenizing your Muslim students?"

Ms. Robert explains, "Three things: First, I never single out Muslim students to explain or defend their experiences. They contribute when they choose to, like any other student. Second, I make sure Muslim voices are part of our regular curriculum, not just during 'diversity units.' And third, I prepare all my students to engage respectfully across difference. We practice listening, asking good questions, and connecting rather than comparing. So, when these conversations happen, everyone knows how to participate thoughtfully. It took trial and error over five years to get here. I made mistakes—put students on the spot, used problematic texts, let discussions get uncomfortable in bad ways. But I kept learning, kept adjusting."

"What would you say to teachers who are afraid to mess up?"

Ms. Robert pauses, considering. "Perfection isn't the goal. Growth is. My Muslim students would rather have teachers who try imperfectly than teachers who avoid the topic entirely."

"Any specific resources that helped?"

"Three things transformed my practice: reading actual Muslim American literature instead of books about Muslims written by non-Muslims; joining teacher networks where Muslim educators share their perspectives; and most importantly, listening to my students when they tell me what works and what doesn't."

"Same curriculum?" Ms. Smith asks.

"Different texts, same approach. Today we're looking at code-switching in Sandra Cisneros. Different identity, same human complexities."

 **Think About It!**

Questions for Reflective Analysis:

1. How did gender stereotypes about Muslim women and men manifest differently across the elementary, middle, and high school cases, and what assumptions were challenged in each scenario?
2. What approaches helped normalize Muslim women's agency and participation without positioning them as either victims or exceptions?
3. How did the intersection of gender with other aspects of identity (race, class, age) create unique challenges for the Muslim students in these cases?
4. What gender-conscious classroom practices from these cases could you adapt for your own teaching context, and how would you modify them for your specific student population?

5. Where do you notice your own assumptions about Muslim gender dynamics in these scenarios, and how might these biases influence your interactions with Muslim students?

 Classroom Strategies and Activities

Strategy 1: Reframing Gender Narratives in Your Curriculum
Standard curriculum materials often perpetuate limiting stereotypes about Muslim gender experiences. Counter these narratives by intentionally curating materials that show the diversity of Muslim gender expressions across time, geography, and individual choice. Create a historical timeline featuring Muslim women leaders throughout history—from Khadijah bint Khuwaylid (successful businesswoman and wife of Prophet Muhammad) to contemporary figures like Ibtihaj Muhammad. Display this timeline alongside other historical references in your classroom, normalizing Muslim women's leadership rather than treating it as exceptional.

You can also integrate profiles of contemporary Muslim professionals across gender expressions into relevant subject areas—scientists during STEM units, authors during literature studies, athletes during physical education. These regular integrations help students see Muslim individuals beyond religious contexts while challenging assumptions about gender-restricted career paths. When teaching subjects with gender dimensions, include diverse Muslim perspectives alongside other viewpoints. During discussions of gender equality movements, for example, include materials on Islamic feminism alongside Western feminist traditions, highlighting how Muslim women have advocated for rights within religious frameworks rather than assuming secularism is required for gender equality.

Project: Gender Beyond Binaries Students investigate how gender is understood in diverse Muslim communities worldwide, examining how different cultural, geographical, and theological contexts create varied gender experiences. They explore questions like: How do Malaysian Muslim women's experiences differ from Egyptian or American Muslim women's experiences? How do Muslim men in different contexts express masculinity? How do some Muslim communities understand gender beyond male/female binaries? Students create comparative analyses that highlight diversity while identifying patterns across contexts.

Strategy 2: Creating Dialogue Spaces for Exploring Gender

Classroom discussions about gender across cultural contexts require thoughtful facilitation that prevents both stereotyping and tokenization while encouraging authentic exchange. Implement structured discussion protocols that prevent putting Muslim students on the spot to explain their religious practices. The "Text-to-Self-to-World" protocol, for example, begins with private reflection before moving to paired and then whole-group discussion, allowing all students to process their thoughts before speaking. This approach creates space for Muslim students to participate authentically rather than as cultural representatives.

It is also critical to be intentional in developing nuanced discussion prompts that move beyond simplistic comparisons of "Western" versus "Muslim" gender practices. Instead of asking "Why do Muslim women wear hijab?", frame questions like "How do people across different cultural contexts express religious identity through clothing?" This approach contextualizes Muslim practices within broader human patterns rather than exceptionalizing them. Establish clear guidelines for discussing potentially sensitive topics, emphasizing that personal opinions about religious practices should be expressed respectfully. Create space for multiple perspectives while maintaining that all students deserve dignity, regardless of their gender expressions or religious identities.

Project: Gendered Media Analysis Lab Students develop critical media literacy skills by analyzing how gender is portrayed across cultural contexts. Using a lab format, student teams collect media examples portraying Muslim men and women, analyze patterns using structured protocols, and create alternative representations that challenge stereotypes. The lab approach emphasizes systematic analysis rather than opinion-based discussion, creating safer engagement with potentially sensitive topics.

Strategy 3: Gender-Conscious Classroom Practices
Everyday classroom routines and interactions either reinforce or challenge limiting gender stereotypes. Implementing gender-conscious practices creates more equitable learning environments for Muslim students. Practice structured role rotations in group activities to ensure all students develop diverse skills regardless of gender. In science labs, project planning, or discussion groups, assign roles systematically rather than allowing students to default to gender-stereotypical positions. This approach creates opportunities for Muslim students to practice leadership, technical skills, or public speaking that societal stereotypes might otherwise limit.

It can also be helpful and reflective to practice observation mapping to track patterns in your own attention, feedback, and expectations across student gender and religious identity. For one week, note which students you call on, whose behavior you monitor, and how you distribute challenging questions. Analyzing this data reveals unconscious biases and helps develop more equitable teaching patterns. Similar to what was discussed in Chapter 3, curating visual displays that normalize diverse gender expressions across cultural contexts can be very impactful. Include images of Muslim men and women in various professional, academic, athletic, and leadership roles alongside other diverse representations. These visual cues shape students' understanding of what's possible across gender and religious identities.

Project: Gender Journey Narratives Students explore how their understanding of gender has evolved through personal experiences, family influences, media exposure, and educational opportunities. Through written reflections, visual timelines, or digital storytelling, they map their gender journeys—significant moments that shaped their understanding of gender roles and expectations. This project normalizes the idea that everyone navigates gender identity development, creating space for

Muslim students to explore their experiences without being singled out.

 School-Wide Implementation

Policy Advocacy Through Demonstrated Need

School policies around dress codes, physical education requirements, and extracurricular participation often unintentionally create barriers for Muslim students navigating gendered religious practices. Teachers can advocate for policy changes most effectively when they document specific impacts on student participation and achievement. Gathering data on how current policies affect Muslim students across genders creates convincing cases for change. You will likely be able to gather how the lack of modest uniform options prevents several female Muslim students from participating fully in sports, which can then help build a successful case for policy revision that improves participation rates without requiring a confrontational approach.

Also, I've experienced that identifying allies among colleagues, administrators, and families strengthens advocacy efforts. Teachers who have successfully accommodated Muslim students' gender-related religious practices can share implementation strategies that address common concerns about practicality, equity, and educational standards.

Strategic Family Partnerships

Building relationships with Muslim families creates invaluable insights into how gender expectations vary across different Muslim communities and how students sometimes navigate differing expectations between home and school. These partnerships require moving beyond assumptions about Muslim family structures to recognize the diversity of gender dynamics within Muslim households. Creating multiple engagement pathways acknowledges diverse family situations. Some Muslim parents may be recent immigrants working multiple jobs, while others may be third-generation professionals with flexible schedules. Offering various participation options—from evening events to digital feedback opportunities to classroom volunteering—ensures that diverse family perspectives inform school approaches to gender.

Engaging Muslim fathers in school partnerships challenges stereotypes about gender roles in Muslim families. Many Muslim fathers are deeply involved in their children's education but may feel unwelcome or unneeded in school settings due to assumptions about patriarchal family structures. Creating specific opportunities for paternal involvement diversifies family representation while challenging limiting stereotypes.

Conclusion

The intersection of gender and Muslim identity creates unique challenges and opportunities in educational settings that demand thoughtful, nuanced responses from educators. Moving beyond the dominant narrative that oscillates between portraying Muslim women as oppressed victims and Muslim men as threatening or controlling requires intentional effort to introduce complexity, diversity, and authentic representation.

From the hypervisibility of hijabi female students to the stereotyping of Muslim boys, gender creates distinct pathways of experience that shape students' sense of belonging, academic engagement, and identity development. The paradox where Muslim students are simultaneously hypervisible through stereotypes yet invisible in their full humanity creates particular challenges during formative educational years. The strategies and case studies shared here—diversifying representations, creating gender-inclusive environments, and addressing gendered Islamophobia—provide practical approaches for transforming educational spaces. When implemented thoughtfully, these strategies create environments where Muslim students can explore their identities without facing reductive stereotypes or feeling pressure to represent their entire religious community.

The work of creating these gender-inclusive environments is ongoing and evolving. It requires educators to continue learning, reflecting on their practices, and adapting to the changing needs of their students.

Resources for Teachers and School Leaders

Academic and Professional Development Resources

- Mir, S. (2014). *Muslim American women on campus: Undergraduate social life and identity.* University of North Carolina Press.
- Hammer, J. (2012). *American Muslim women, religious authority, and activism.* University of Texas Press.
- Abo-Zena, M. M., & Tabbah, R. (2017). *Muslim American women in campus communities.* Journal of Muslim Mental Health, 11(1).

School Policy and Implementation Guides

- Muslim Public Affairs Council (MPAC): "Inclusion of American Muslims" school guide
- Department of Education: "Protecting Students from Harassment and Hate Crime" guidance

Books Featuring Diverse Muslim Gender Experiences

- Muhammad, I., & Ali, S. K. (2019). *The proudest blue: A story of hijab and family.* Little, Brown Books for Young Readers.
- Zoboi, I. (Ed.). (2019). *Black enough: Stories of being young & black in America.* Balzer + Bray.
- Saeed, A. (2018). *Amal unbound.* Nancy Paulsen Books.

Digital and Online Resources

- Muslimah Media Watch—Critical analysis of Muslim women's representation in media
- "Hijabi Ballers"– Organization celebrating Muslim women in sports
- HEART Women & Girls—Resources for Muslim girls on health and well-being

Community and Support Networks

- Muslim Anti-Racism Collaborative (MuslimARC) — Intersectional resources addressing gender and race
- Muslim Women's Alliance—Mentorship programs and support networks

Curriculum and Classroom Materials

- Learning for Justice (formerly Teaching Tolerance): "Gender Equity in the Classroom" resources
- PBS LearningMedia: "Women in Islam" collection
- National Women's History Museum: Digital resources on women's contributions across cultural contexts

5
Amplifying Counter-Narratives

"I wanted people to know, yes, I am Muslim. We're not crazy; we're normal people."—Yasmine

Introduction

Counter-narratives hold profound significance for sharing authentic Muslim experiences. The stories Muslim Americans tell about themselves often contrast sharply with mainstream narratives about Islam and Muslims in America. These counter-narratives challenge stereotypes, illuminate lived realities, and reclaim the power of self-definition. For Muslim students, encountering authentic representations of their experiences in educational settings powerfully validates their identities and sense of belonging. The importance of counter-narratives is magnified by the pervasiveness of misleading stereotypes about Muslims in American media and popular culture. As one student in my research shared, "non-Muslims don't know enough about Islam. They only believe what's shown in the media." These distorted representations often portray Muslims as monolithic, potentially threatening, fundamentally foreign, or incompatible with American values. Such narratives impact not only how others perceive Muslim students but also how Muslim youth understand themselves.

The absence of authentic Muslim voices in curriculum and educational discourse may lead Muslim students to internalize the message that their experiences and perspectives are not valued in educational spaces. I'll share a personal story from a time during my doctoral program. Each term we were asked to introduce ourselves, and my introduction usually went something like this, "Hi, I'm Noor, I'm originally from Pakistan, and I work at a faith-based school in Massachusetts." It took me four terms of saying this as a self-introduction to recognize the ways I was minimizing and invalidating myself. Saying that I was originally from Pakistan, is a (not so) muted way of sanitizing myself and making my identity palatable for a predominantly White American audience; it's akin to saying, "hey, I'm safe, I'm no longer in or from Pakistan, I only originated there," and saying that I worked at a faith-based school and not a Muslim school, is akin to saying "let's make myself relevant, by diffusing my own edges, blur myself to something more generic, or make myself more compatible, because who will care for the experience of a Muslim school teacher; it's too niche and loses relevance, but if I say faith-based or non-public, then more colleagues would be able to resonate and listen." The major realization for me was that this self-invalidation, making myself small to fit into a box, was not a choice I was making after deep contemplation. I was making it on autopilot, as if it was only expected, like that is what I had been trained for all my life. This was a pivotal moment for me and I was shaken by this realization and how the way I performed hadn't just crept up on me but had been perpetuated and normalized. I was 36 years old at the time, in a doctoral program, an academic space; I had children of my own; I had two Masters—and all my life experiences and education had still landed me in this way of being. I wondered what then the life and educational experience of a 6-year-old, or a 16-year-old was. How were Muslim kindergartners and middle schoolers navigating their identities, what burdens were they carrying, what did they see in themselves through what the system was teaching them?

Here's the thing: when you don't see yourself represented, you begin to stop seeing yourself.

Here's the other thing: the danger is not that if you don't tell your story, no one will tell your story. The greater danger is that if you don't tell your story, someone else will tell your story. And that version of your story is one that has been hijacked by white telling; it runs the very real risk of being superficial, convenient, and conforming of stereotypes that perpetuate monolithic narratives. That's why counter-narratives are a deeply powerful tool, because they place the stories in the hands of the people whose stories they are.

Counter-narratives serve multiple functions in educational settings. They provide Muslim students with the opportunity to reflect upon their own experiences, affirming their identities and sense of belonging, while also providing perspective to non-Muslim students about diverse Muslim experiences, expanding their understanding beyond stereotypical representations, developing empathy and cross-cultural understanding. As Sana shared in my research, "I've never felt myself represented in the curriculum and wished that there had been more inclusive education about Ramadhan and Eid so people would know more about their Muslim classmates."

The educational significance of counter-narratives extends beyond representation to also encompass cognitive justice—the recognition that different ways of knowing and understanding the world are valid and valuable. When Muslim counter-narratives are excluded from educational discourse, Muslim students experience the devaluation of their knowledge and interpretive frameworks. Including counter-narratives helps create more epistemically just learning environments where diverse knowledge systems are recognized and valued.

This chapter urges us to consider how educators can amplify Muslim counter-narratives in educational settings, creating spaces where authentic Muslim voices challenge stereotypes, illuminate diverse lived realities, and contribute to more comprehensive understanding. By centering Muslim counter-narratives, educators acknowledge the expertise of experience that Muslim students and communities bring to educational spaces, creating environments where all students benefit from richer, more complex understanding of Muslim American experiences.

Framing our Conversation

The concept of counter-narratives emerges from Critical Race Theory (CRT), which recognizes the power of stories in challenging dominant narratives that perpetuate inequality. As pioneered by scholars like Derrick Bell (1992), Richard Delgado (1995), and Kimberlé Crenshaw (1991), CRT positions counter-storytelling as a methodological tool for illuminating marginalized experiences and challenging mainstream assumptions. For Muslim Americans, counter-narratives serve similar functions in contesting dominant portrayals and reclaiming narrative agency. Edward Said (1978) emphasized Western discourse has historically constructed the "Orient" and its peoples as exotic, threatening, backward, and fundamentally "other." These Orientalist tropes continue to shape contemporary representations of Muslims, positioning them as inherently foreign to American society. Counter-narratives challenge these constructions by presenting complex, authentic Muslim American experiences that defy simplistic categorization.

For Muslim students, encountering counter-narratives that affirm the value of their religious and cultural identities supports positive identity development, sense of belonging and overall academic experience. When these counter-narratives also examine how anti-Muslim racism operates historically and institutionally, they help develop students' critical consciousness about social inequities affecting Muslim communities.

Reflective Practice

For educators committed to amplifying Muslim counter-narratives, reflection must begin with examining our own relationship to narrative authority. Begin by considering whose stories you tend to prioritize in your personal understanding and professional practice. Do you unconsciously give more weight to dominant cultural narratives about Muslims, or do you actively seek out and value Muslim voices speaking for themselves? Notice patterns in whose perspectives you share with students and colleagues.

Reflect on your own experiences with counter-narratives. When has hearing directly from a marginalized community changed your understanding of an issue? How did that experience differ from learning about that community through mainstream sources? Conversely, when have you felt misrepresented by others telling your story and how did that misrepresentation impact you? These personal experiences can help develop empathy for Muslim students whose lived realities are frequently misrepresented in dominant narratives.

Consider the narrative ecosystem of your classroom and curriculum. Which Muslim stories are present, and which are absent? When Muslim experiences appear, are they presented through Muslim voices or through external perspectives? Are Muslims portrayed primarily in historical or religious contexts, or are contemporary, everyday Muslim American experiences represented? Are Muslim counter-narratives positioned as equally valid ways of knowing, or are they treated as subjective opinions compared to "objective" dominant narratives? Regular audit of these patterns helps identify opportunities to amplify authentic Muslim voices.

Examine how power dynamics influence narrative exchange in your educational space. When Muslim students share their experiences, how do you and others respond? Are their stories met with genuine engagement, or with defensiveness, skepticism, or tokenization? Do Muslim students feel pressure to present "acceptable" narratives that conform to non-Muslim or mainstream expectations? Notice whether Muslim students are positioned as representatives of their entire religion or community, rather than as individuals with unique perspectives.

Reflect on your approach to facilitating counter-narratives. When introducing Muslim narratives that challenge dominant perspectives, how do you prepare students to engage respectfully? What frameworks do you provide for understanding these narratives within broader historical and social contexts? How do you balance creating space for authentic Muslim voices while protecting Muslim students from becoming the focus of potentially difficult discussions?

 Putting it into Action

Current Event Case Study: Civic Education Through Contemporary Counter-Narratives

High school civics teacher Elena Santos transformed her unit on local government when Zohran Mamdani, a Muslim American state assemblyman, announced his candidacy for New York City mayor. As Islamophobic attacks against Mamdani appeared in media and social platforms, Elena recognized an authentic teaching opportunity about both civic engagement and counter-narratives. "Students were seeing in real time how a candidate's religious identity was being weaponized," Elena explains. "I didn't plan this unit—it emerged organically when students started asking questions about news coverage they were seeing."

Elena restructured her local government unit to incorporate analysis of media coverage of Mamdani's campaign. Students tracked mainstream news articles, social media discussions, and campaign materials, identifying narrative patterns in how Mamdani's Muslim identity was framed in different contexts.

What made the unit particularly powerful was examining Mamdani's own counter-narrative strategies. Students analyzed his speeches, interviews, and social media where he directly addressed anti-Muslim attacks while reframing the conversation toward policy issues and community needs. They noted his refusal to downplay his Muslim identity while also resisting being defined solely through a religious lens. "This wasn't just about analyzing discrimination—it was about studying effective resistance through narrative control," Elena notes. "Students saw a Muslim American political figure actively reshaping public discourse rather than simply responding to attacks."

The most transformative classroom moments came when students compared Mamdani's experience to historical patterns of religious and racial othering in American politics. They researched the anti-Catholic rhetoric during John F. Kennedy's campaign, anti-Semitic attacks against Jewish candidates, and racialized coverage of candidates of color, identifying both continuities and unique aspects of anti-Muslim political narratives.

When students expressed interest in taking their learning beyond analysis, Elena helped them develop a Voter Education Guide on Media Literacy that taught community members how to recognize religious bias in political coverage. "The Mamdani campaign gave us a living case study in counter-narrative creation," Elena reflects. "Students weren't just learning abstract concepts—they were watching counter-narratives unfold in real time and analyzing their effectiveness, all while developing deeper understanding of both democratic processes and media representation."

Elementary Teacher Story: The Journal Project Revolution

Fourth-grade teacher Miguel Gonzalez never planned to challenge stereotypes through journaling—he just wanted to improve his students' writing skills. But when 9-year-old Amina wrote, "People think Muslims are scary but we're just normal kids," Miguel recognized an opportunity to create space for counter-narratives within his existing literacy curriculum. Miguel had always included daily journaling in his classroom routine, using simple prompts to build writing fluency. After Amina's entry, he began occasionally incorporating prompts that invited personal experience sharing: "Write about a time when someone misunderstood something about you" or "Describe a tradition that's important to your family."

"I wasn't asking specifically about religious identity," Miguel explains. "But these open-ended prompts created space for students to share aspects of their lives that rarely appeared in our curriculum. Muslim students began writing about Ramadhan dinners, Eid celebrations, and mosque visits—ordinary childhood experiences that happened to involve their faith." The journal entries revealed how even young Muslim students were aware of stereotypes about their communities. Amina wrote about a store clerk watching her mother suspiciously. Ibrahim described feeling nervous whenever Islam was mentioned in class. These entries demonstrated that elementary students were already navigating complex narrative terrains around identity.

Miguel adapted his approach based on what emerged from the journals. When students wrote about misunderstandings they'd experienced, he began offering the option to develop these journal entries into more polished personal narratives that could be shared with classmates if there was willingness to share. "The most powerful aspect was how ordinary these counter-narratives felt within our classroom routine," Miguel notes. "They weren't special diversity lessons, they were just part of our regular writing practice, which normalized Muslim experiences alongside everyone else's stories."

The journal project eventually evolved into a class book called Our Real Lives, featuring students writing about their diverse experiences. Each student contributed several pages, creating a collective counter-narrative to the limited representations in their textbooks. The book became a favorite in the classroom library, with students regularly choosing it during independent reading time.

Middle School Subject-Specific Approach: Science Class Redefined

When seventh-grade science teacher Aisha Jackson noticed her Muslim students disengaging during the history of science unit, she decided to investigate why. "I discovered our curriculum presented science history entirely through a Western European lens," Aisha explains. "The only time Muslims appeared was a brief mention of 'knowledge preservation' during the European Dark Ages—as if Muslims merely held Greek knowledge until Europeans could reclaim it."

Rather than requesting curriculum revision permission, Aisha began incorporating Scientist Spotlight segments into her regular instruction. Each week, she dedicated 10 minutes to highlighting scientists from diverse backgrounds, including Muslim scientists both historical and contemporary. These spotlights weren't add-ons, they connected directly to the content students were learning, showing how scientific knowledge develops across cultures and time periods.

"I started with historical figures like Ibn al-Haytham when teaching optics and Al-Khwarizmi when covering mathematical concepts," Aisha notes. "But the most powerful counter-narratives came from featuring contemporary Muslim scientists like chemist Ahmed Zewail or NASA engineer Hibah Rahmani, who directly challenged the notion that modern science is primarily a Western endeavor." Aisha carefully framed these spotlights not as "diverse additions" but as corrections to an incomplete narrative. "I explicitly told students, 'We're filling gaps in our typical science story to get a more accurate picture of how scientific knowledge actually develops.' This framing helped students understand that counter-narratives enhance accuracy rather than pushing an agenda."

The impact became evident when students began independently researching scientists from their own cultural backgrounds. Muslim students showed renewed engagement, often bringing information about scientific contributions connected to their heritage. "Rayyan brought articles about modern Pakistani physicists. Samira researched Algerian mathematicians. They were suddenly seeing themselves in science—not as tokens, but as part of a continuous tradition of contribution."

 **Think About It!**

Questions for Reflective Analysis:
- How do these approaches create space for counter-narratives while avoiding putting Muslim students in the position of representing their entire faith?
- What makes counter-narrative work different from general inclusion or diversity initiatives?
- How might these approaches be adapted for different subject areas or age groups?

♦ What resources would you need to implement similar counter-narrative approaches in your educational context?

 Classroom Strategies and Activities

When implementing counter-narrative strategies in educational settings, it's critical to center authentic Muslim American voices and experiences. While texts like Khaled Hosseini's *The Kite Runner* and Malala Yousafzai's *I Am Malala* have become staples in many classrooms, they problematically position Muslims as belonging only in faraway lands, portray protagonists as exceptional precisely because they differ from their "backward" communities, and reinforce white saviorism by having Western intervention "rescue" these characters and bring them to the Western world for liberation and opportunity. Such narratives, despite their perceived inclusivity, actually reinforce harmful stereotypes about Muslims while allowing educators to believe they're promoting diversity. True counter-narratives must center Muslims as belonging fully in Western contexts and avoid exoticizing or otherizing Muslim experiences.

The following classroom strategies help educators amplify authentic Muslim counter-narratives that challenge dominant stereotypes while creating more inclusive learning environments.

Strategy 1: Critical Media Analysis: Unpacking Dominant Narratives
Most students have absorbed thousands of media images about Muslims before they ever enter our classrooms. These accumulated representations shape their understanding—often unconsciously—creating narrative frameworks that seem natural rather than constructed. Often our students can't recognize stereotypes about Muslims because they have nothing to compare them to. They need analytical tools to see these patterns and understand how they're created in the first place and teaching students to identify dominant narratives about Muslims requires concrete analysis techniques. Guide students through close

reading of news articles, textbook passages, television clips, and social media posts, looking for specific patterns: Are Muslims portrayed primarily in contexts of conflict? Do Muslim women appear as lacking agency? Are Muslims positioned as inherently foreign to American society? This can help students recognize how seemingly neutral media constructs particular views of Muslims.

Another important piece to consider here is developing students' understanding of narrative authority—who gets to tell stories and whose perspectives are deemed credible. When analyzing news coverage, have students tracked whose voices are quoted, whether Muslims speak for themselves or are spoken about, and what expertise Muslims are permitted to claim. This analysis often reveals that even stories about Muslim communities frequently marginalize actual Muslim perspectives.

Project Idea: Students can create Narrative Deconstruction Portfolios documenting dominant narratives they identify in various media sources. These portfolios include annotated examples, analysis of patterns across different sources, and reflections on how these narratives shape public understanding. By collecting concrete evidence of problematic representations, students develop more sophisticated awareness of how narratives function.

Strategy 2: Counter-Narrative Immersion: Beyond Token Representation

Counter-narratives thrive when we move beyond isolated diversity selections to create immersive environments where authentic Muslim voices appear regularly across the curriculum. Realizing that often times Muslim representation is limited to sections in cultural diversity can be transformational, as one can then be more intentional about creating narrative integration points throughout the year—places where Muslim authors and characters appear naturally in units on various themes and genres, not just when we're explicitly discussing cultural difference.

Contemporary Muslim American literature offers rich counter-narratives that challenge stereotypes through complex characterization rather than direct argument. Works like S. K. Ali's *Saints and Misfits*, Tahereh Mafi's *A Very Large Expanse of Sea*, and Sabaa Tahir's *All My Rage* feature Muslim American teenagers navigating universal adolescent challenges while also dealing with Islamophobia and cultural complexity. These texts provide both windows for non-Muslim students and mirrors for Muslim students, creating more authentic representation than works focusing on Muslims in foreign contexts.

Short-form counter-narratives can also transform daily classroom routines with minimal disruption to existing plans. Daily poetry readings might include works by Kazim Ali, Mohja Kahf, or Naomi Shihab Nye. Journal prompts might incorporate quotes from Muslim thinkers across various fields. Current events discussions might feature reporting by Muslim American journalists. These brief but consistent exposures normalize Muslim voices as part of the intellectual landscape rather than exotic additions. Narrative hospitality—making space for stories that challenge our existing frameworks—becomes essential when introducing counter-narratives that may provoke resistance. Help students develop practices of suspending judgment, listening for understanding rather than agreement, asking genuine questions rather than challenging others' experiences, and sitting with discomfort rather than dismissing unfamiliar perspectives.

Project Idea: Students themselves often discover powerful counter-narratives once they know what to look for. Create physical or digital spaces where students can share articles, videos, artwork, or social media content created by Muslims that challenges stereotypes they've encountered. Encourage students to briefly explain why each contribution matters, creating an annotated collection that grows throughout the year. This student-curated approach builds collective resources while developing students' critical awareness.

Strategy 3: Student Voice Studio: From Analysis to Creation

When students create their own counter-narratives, they develop not just critical analysis skills but the capacity to reshape discourse through their own voices. The most powerful counter-narratives don't directly argue against stereotypes, instead, they tell rich, specific stories that simply make stereotypes impossible to maintain in the face of complex reality. Poetry and creative writing provide alternative avenues for counter-narrative expression. Students can develop personal narratives, fictional pieces featuring Muslim characters, or research-based creative work exploring historical Muslim figures. These literary approaches allow exploration of complex emotions and experiences that might be difficult to address in academic formats, while developing students' writerly voices and creative techniques.

For counter-narrative work to be ethical, it must respect Muslim students' agency in determining whether and how to share their experiences. Create multiple options for participation, including research-based projects that don't require personal disclosure, fictional approaches that allow exploration of issues through created characters, and anonymous contribution options. Explicitly discuss the difference between Muslim students sharing their own experiences versus non-Muslim students attempting to represent Muslim experiences, emphasizing that allies amplify rather than speak for others.

Project Idea: Digital storytelling offers accessible formats for counter-narrative creation. Students might create short documentaries about Muslim community members, personal video essays exploring aspects of their identities, or social media campaigns challenging specific misconceptions. These multimedia approaches develop technical skills while creating shareable content that can reach broader audiences. For Muslim students who choose to share their experiences, these projects provide platforms for authentic self-representation; for non-Muslim students, they offer opportunities to amplify rather than appropriate Muslim voices.

School-Wide Implementation

Teacher-to-Teacher Influence

Some of the most profound school culture changes happen through peer relationships among educators, where successful classroom approaches spread organically through professional networks. Informal sharing can be more powerful than formal professional development. When one math teacher incorporates profiles of contemporary Muslim mathematicians into her classroom, colleagues are likely to notice student engagement increasing and ask about her approach. Creating simple Mathematical Spotlight handouts featuring these mathematicians that other teachers could immediately use, can result in these appearing in classrooms throughout the math department without requiring formal curriculum revision.

Cross-subject collaboration creates natural pathways for counter-narrative expansion. When literature and history teachers coordinate their treatment of particular time periods, science and art teachers develop interconnected units on innovation across cultures, or physical education and health teachers collaborate on culturally responsive wellness approaches, counter-narratives can flow across disciplinary boundaries. These collaborative relationships create multiple entry points for authentic Muslim voices throughout students' educational experience.

Student Leadership as Cultural Catalyst

Teacher-supported affinity groups provide vital spaces for developing and sharing counter-narratives. Muslim Student Associations, with appropriate faculty support, can create powerful educational resources that reach the broader school community. Cross-group collaborations amplify counter-narrative impact as well. When Muslim student organizations partner with journalism classes, art clubs, debate teams, or student government, they reach broader audiences while building coalitions. These collaborations help all participating students recognize interconnections between different forms of marginalization while creating more nuanced understandings of Muslim experiences.

The most sustainable counter-narrative initiatives equip students with specific skills for narrative development and sharing. Rather than just encouraging general expression, provide structured opportunities for students to learn interviewing techniques, digital storytelling methods, ethical approaches to sharing others' stories, and effective ways to address misconceptions. These transferable skills empower students to continue counter-narrative work beyond specific school projects.

Conclusion

Amplifying Muslim counter-narratives transforms educational environments from spaces where stereotypical representations predominate to communities where authentic Muslim voices are valued and integrated. We must commit to abandoning performative approaches for true inclusion of diverse voices.

The classroom strategies, school-wide implementation ideas, and case studies showcase how incorporating authentic Muslim voices across the curriculum, facilitating student-created counter-narratives, and developing critical media literacy offer concrete approaches for amplifying Muslim counter-narratives while building all students' capacity for critical engagement with diverse perspectives. They help create learning environments where Muslim experiences are normalized rather than exoticized, where stereotypes are challenged through authentic representation, and where students develop skills for critically evaluating media messages about Muslims. By implementing these approaches, educators can help create educational environments where Muslim students experience true belonging rather than perpetual othering. In these environments, Muslim students can share their authentic experiences and perspectives, contributing to educational discourse not as tokens or representatives but as valued members of diverse learning communities.

Resources for Teachers and School Leaders

Academic and Professional Development Resources

- ◆ Paris, D., & Alim, H. S. (Eds.). (2017). *Culturally sustaining pedagogies: Teaching and learning for justice in a changing world*. Teachers College Press.

- Tindongan, C. W. (2011). Negotiating Muslim youth identity in a post-9/11 world. *The High School Journal*, 95(1), 72–87.
- Ahmad, I., & Szpara, M. Y. (2003). Muslim children in urban America: The New York City schools experience. *Journal of Muslim Minority Affairs*, 23(2), 295–301.

Curriculum and Classroom Materials

- StoryCorps: Oral history collection archives including Muslim American stories
- PBS: Documentaries and educational resources on the Muslim American experience
- Narrative 4: Story exchange program for building empathy across differences

School Policy and Implementation Guides

- National Council for the Social Studies: "Guidelines for Teaching About Religion"
- Media Literacy Now: Implementation guides for schools on developing critical media literacy
- Center for Media Literacy: Education frameworks and resources

Books Offering Muslim Counter-Narratives

- Wilson, G. W. (2013). *Ms. Marvel* series. Marvel Comics.
- Ali, S. K. (2019). *Love from A to Z*. Salaam Reads.
- Kahf, M. (2006). *The girl in the tangerine scarf*. PublicAffairs.

Digital and Online Resources

- Muslim Public Affairs Council (MPAC): Media literacy resources

- Muslim Matters—Platform for Muslim writers to share their perspectives
- The Institute for Social Policy and Understanding (ISPU): Research and resources for young Muslims

Community and Support Networks

- We Need Diverse Books—Resources for young writers from underrepresented communities
- Youth Radio/YR Media—Training program for youth journalists
- Unity Productions Foundation: Film and education resources on Muslim narratives

6

Examining Cultural Norms in Educational Environments

"The reason why I haven't felt discrimination is because I pass off as white."—Hafsa

Introduction

My son jokingly began calling himself Kevin in high school, a name that conveniently stuck with him for a while. Our names are considered difficult, they roll differently on the tongue, and one will often see others use a language of violence as they offer a smiling apology at mispronouncing them and announcing that that amount of effort was all they could invest in this exercise, "I'm sorry I butchered your name." Each time I am at the doctor's office the expression on the nurse's face as she looks at Noorulsabah Ali is my cue that she is looking for me. Mohammad loses his syllables to become Mo, Yusuf steps on white soil and shapeshifts to Joseph, all for the comfort of maintaining the white norm. I recall the time when I was invited to serve on the board of a town-wide mental health organization and explicitly was told it was for increasing diversity, only to find out after I had obliged that a seat at the table absolutely does not mean a

DOI: 10.4324/9781003613602-6

voice at the table. The brown opinion matters less or not at all in spaces that continue to tokenize diversity but remain invested in colonial control. We often find ourselves in precarious situations where we take on opportunities for the purposes of representation and then realize that it was only our colored presence that was needed and not anything more. That opinions and analysis are only trusted and valued if it passes the pigmentation test. This work is draining because it is muted so often, because it is slowed down to the pace of white comfort, and because it is disallowed authentic engagement until it has first proved itself worthy, exceptional, safe, and friendly all at once.

In critical race theory, whiteness refers not simply to racial identity but to a cultural system that establishes norms, values, and ways of knowing as universal standards. Whiteness functions as property, conferring access, legitimacy, and belonging to those who can approximate its cultural markers while excluding those who cannot. In educational settings, whiteness operates as the invisible standard against which all other cultures are measured, making white ways of learning, communicating, and demonstrating knowledge appear natural and neutral rather than culturally specific. For Muslim American students, this means their religious knowledge systems, cultural practices, and ways of being are consistently positioned as deviations from an unmarked white norm. The closer they can approximate whiteness through names, appearance, cultural expressions, or religious visibility, the greater their access to educational belonging and success.

Whiteness often functions as both property and the default standard in American educational spaces conferring privileges, protections, and belonging to those who possess it. Muslim American students find themselves navigating a landscape where their cultural knowledge and religious identity are systematically devalued or rendered invisible. So, Hafsa's statement about "passing" reveals a profound reality that many Muslim American students understand viscerally: proximity to whiteness provides safety. Those who can assimilate to white cultural norms or whose physical appearance allows them to "pass", gain access to privileges unavailable to their visibly Muslim peers.

This dynamic creates painful choices between authentic religious expression and social acceptance impacting academic success.

Muslim American students experience this tenet's impact in multiple dimensions. They encounter curriculum that positions Western knowledge as universal while treating Islamic perspectives as particular, awkward, irrelevant, inferior, or exotic. They navigate institutional spaces designed around white Christian-centric norms that treat Muslim practices as deviations requiring special accommodation. They face assessment systems that privilege white Western modes of knowledge demonstration while devaluing alternative approaches. As one student in my research noted, "We are considered not American enough," capturing how whiteness establishes boundaries around who can claim full belonging in educational spaces.

For Muslim Americans, whose religious identity is frequently racialized regardless of their ethnic background, this creates a particular form of exclusion from the property benefits of whiteness. This exclusion has intensified in the post-9/11 landscape, where Muslims are frequently portrayed as fundamentally incompatible with American identity. This chapter examines how Muslim American students experience and navigate educational spaces dominated by white cultural norms. More importantly, it explores how educators can challenge these dynamics to create learning environments where diverse cultural capital is recognized and valued, where multiple knowledge systems are treated as legitimate, and where Muslim students can fully belong without surrendering their religious and cultural identities.

Framing our Conversation

Whiteness shapes our educational spaces in ways often invisible to those who benefit from it. Yet, it presents itself as an entire system that treats certain ways of being, knowing, and expressing as inherently valuable while marking others as foreign, deficient, or problematic. When a Muslim student changes their name to something "more American" or when an Islamic studies student is asked "but what practical skills will you learn?" we're witnessing whiteness functioning as property. This concept, brilliantly articulated by legal scholar Cheryl Harris, helps us understand how whiteness became something people could possess, something that delivers actual benefits, protections, and access. For Muslim students, this property system operates through a peculiar kind of racial categorization that transforms religious identity into racial classification.

The years following 9/11 dramatically intensified this dynamic. As Khaled Beydoun documents in his research on American Islamophobia, Muslim identity became increasingly racialized through an organized system of policies, practices, and cultural narratives. In our schools, this manifests when Muslim students find their religious identity hypervisible as a potential security concern yet invisible when it comes to positive representation or cultural recognition. I've watched Muslim students navigate this contradictory position—simultaneously too visible and not visible enough—which requires exhausting emotional and intellectual labor that their peers never face. This labor becomes particularly evident when we consider what Pierre Bourdieu called "cultural capital"—the knowledge, behaviors, and skills that are valued in specific social contexts. Our educational systems don't just teach content; they teach particular ways of speaking, writing, thinking, and being that are treated as neutral and universal. We see Muslim students grapple with this when their multilingualism is treated as a language deficit while their white peers' knowledge of French is celebrated as sophisticated.

The colonial legacy embedded in educational institutions further reinforces these dynamics. Many Muslim American students come from backgrounds with histories deeply marked by European colonization that actively worked to dismantle indigenous knowledge systems while imposing Western frameworks as superior. This colonial mindset persists in contemporary educational practices that treat Western intellectual traditions as universal while positioning non-Western traditions as culturally specific and less rigorous.

Reflective Practice

For educators committed to challenging whiteness as property, reflection begins with examining our own relationship to white cultural norms and how they shape our educational practices. Consider the following reflective questions: What cultural practices and ways of knowing do you instinctively classify as appropriate or academic in educational settings? How might these classifications reflect white Western standards rather than universal values? When have you expected Muslim students to adapt to dominant norms without questioning why these norms predominate?

How might your curriculum choices reinforce whiteness as the default standard of knowledge? Do history courses position Western civilization as the central driver of human progress while treating Islamic contributions as peripheral? Are literature selections primarily drawn from Western literary traditions? Do science lessons acknowledge contributions from Islamic scholars, or do they present Western scientific methods as the only legitimate approach to knowledge or silo these canons as having developed without influence from the Islamic world?

Another area to evaluate is how assessment practices might favor white cultural expressions. Do your evaluation metrics value particular communication styles, argumentation approaches, or demonstration methods that align with white Western traditions? What forms of cultural knowledge might these approaches fail to recognize? How might you expand assessment to recognize diverse ways of demonstrating understanding?

Reflect on your responses to expressions of Islamic knowledge in educational settings. When Muslim students draw on religious knowledge in academic contexts, do you treat these contributions as valuable or as inappropriate insertions of religion into secular spaces? Do you recognize Islamic scholarship as intellectually rigorous, or do you subtly communicate that Western academic traditions are more legitimate? Finally, examine your reaction to criticisms of white cultural dominance. When conversations about curriculum inclusivity or institutional practices arise, do you feel defensive? Can you identify what about these conversations triggers discomfort?

 Putting it into Action

Elementary: The Names We Carry

Ms. Elena Reyes kept a pronunciation guide on her desk. Twenty-three years of teaching kindergarten in increasingly diverse neighborhoods had taught her to prepare. She'd mastered Polish consonant clusters, Vietnamese tones, Spanish regional variations.

Then Ruqayyah walked into her classroom.

"Let me try... Roo-kay-ah?"

The five-year-old's mother smiled that particular smile Elena had seen before. Practiced. Patient. Resigned. "Close enough. Most people just call her Rocky, my mother-in-law always says we should have given her an easier name for America."

Elena carried this conversation with her through her day. During art, she watched Ruqayyah carefully paint each letter of her name on her paper, purple and deliberate.

"Beautiful letters," Elena commented.

"My name means 'rise'," Ruqayyah offered quietly. "Like the sun."

That afternoon, Elena found herself thinking about her own grandmother, María Elena, who became Mary Ellen at the factory, never correcting anyone. The way she'd say her full name only at home, like a secret.

The next morning, Elena asked, "Ruqayyah, would you teach me your name correctly?"

What followed was a five-minute tutorial on Arabic phonemes, kindergartener-style. "The 'q' comes from way back here," Ruqayyah demonstrated, pointing to her throat.

"Can we all try?" asked Mike.

Soon twenty kindergarteners were attempting glottal sounds, giggling, trying again. But they were trying. And Ruqayyah? She stood a little taller.

It became part of their routine because we teach them to read 'through' and 'enough', and names shouldn't be harder than English spelling rules. By spring, the shift had settled into the classroom's DNA. New students learned quickly: everyone's name mattered here. All four syllables of it.

Middle School: The Palestine Exception

Mr. Mike Thompson had built his eighth-grade social studies class on open dialogue. The walls showcased student essays on everything from local homelessness to global warming. His motto, painted above the whiteboard: "No topic too tough for respectful discussion."

He believed it. Until the day Zaynab raised her hand during current events.

"Mr. T, can we discuss what's happening in Gaza? My cousin's school was—"

"Let's table that for now," Mike heard himself say. "Complex situation. We need to stick to our article schedule."

The words felt wrong leaving his mouth. Just last week, Emma had presented on abortion rights, taking a firmly pro-choice stance, and he'd praised her for brave political engagement. Jackson's presentation on gun control had been equally one-sided, equally passionate, equally welcomed.

But Palestine felt dangerous, somehow.

Tariq caught him after class. Not confrontational, just curious. "Mr. T, why do some current events count more than others?"

Mike didn't have an answer that didn't sound hypocritical. Nine times this semester Muslim students had tried to bring up Palestine. Nine times he'd redirected. "Find more balanced sources." "Consider all perspectives." "Let's avoid controversial politics." Meanwhile, his feedback on other political topics read differently. "Powerful personal connection!" on Maya's immigration essay. "Excellent use of family history!" on Ben's piece about Irish independence.

Mike didn't announce a curriculum revolution. He simply stopped applying different rules. When Amara brought Palestinian poetry to their literature unit, he engaged. When

Kareem's grandfather visited to discuss his memories of 1948, Mike facilitated like any other oral history project.

Some parents complained. The principal "cautioned" him. But Mike noticed something: his Muslim students started participating differently. Not just about Palestine—about everything. As if they'd been holding back, testing whether their full selves were welcome. The discussions weren't always smooth. He had to develop better facilitation skills, learning to navigate the particular tensions this topic carried. But he applied the same standards across all controversial topics. Personal connections were either always valid or never valid. Passion was either always appropriate or always tempered.

No exceptions.

"You know what changed everything?" Zaynab told him during final presentations. "You stopped acting like caring about our families was radical."

High School: The Professional Academic

Ms. Camilla Delgado prided herself on preparing students for college success. Fifteen years of teaching AP English had given her a keen eye for what admissions committees wanted: polished presentations, assertive participation, professional appearance.

She could usually predict who'd get into top schools by October. Then Safiya Patel complicated her metrics.

"Remember," Camilla announced before mock interviews, "professional presentation matters. Dress for the future you want." She noticed Safiya adjust her hijab, saw Hamza glance at his modest clothes. But these were the realities they'd face in college interviews. During presentations, Camilla's practiced rubric worked smoothly. McKenzie earned a top score for her aggressive debate style and sharp blazer. Connor's interruptions showed intellectual leadership.

Then Safiya presented her analysis of code-switching in The Namesake. Her insights connected linguistic theory to immigrant experience. But she spoke quietly, paused between thoughts, rarely held eye contact for more than a moment. Her outfit—an elegantly draped hijab with a long tunic over tailored pants was meticulous but didn't fit Camilla's professional template.

"Stronger eye contact needed," Camilla noted. "Project more authority. Consider a blazer for interviews."

Safiya requested clarification asking, "Ms. Delgado, when you tell me my clothes aren't professional enough, what exactly is unprofessional about them?"

Camilla faltered. "Well, for interviews, you want to look... polished."

"I spent forty minutes on this hijab style. My outfit cost more than McKenzie's. Everything is pressed, coordinated, intentional. So what you mean is I should look less Muslim."

The words hung there. Every behavior coded as "professional" aligned with white Western norms. Loud confidence over quiet authority. Aggressive interruption over thoughtful listening. Fitted clothing over modest dress. Camilla had told Hamza his beard looked "untidy," and suggested Ibrahim's traditional kufi might "send the wrong message."

Camilla considered how she'd straightened her hair and practiced eliminating any trace of Spanish accent to be taken seriously in academia. How she'd internalized those standards so thoroughly she now enforced them. But more importantly, she considered how this required intentional dismantling in her own practice.

 **Think About It!**

Questions for Reflective Analysis:

1. How did each case study reveal different ways that whiteness functions as "property" in educational settings—from linguistic norms to political discourse standards to professional appearance expectations?
2. What specific moments in these cases showed educators recognizing their own investment in white cultural norms? How did this recognition lead to changed practices?

> 3. How do the challenges faced by Ruqayyah (names), Zaynab (Palestine), and Safiya (professional appearance) demonstrate the different "costs" Muslim students pay when they cannot access white cultural capital?
> 4. Which strategies from these cases could help you identify where white norms operate as invisible standards in your own teaching context?
> 5. How might implementing these approaches create resistance from colleagues, parents, or administrators who benefit from current arrangements? What would you need to navigate such challenges?

Classroom Strategies and Activities

Strategy 1: Challenging Language Hierarchies: From Deficit to Asset

Many Muslim students navigate multiple linguistic worlds, speaking heritage languages at home, Arabic for religious purposes, and English at school. Yet our educational systems often treat this multilingualism as a problem to solve rather than a resource to celebrate. You may notice a pattern when some students may be utilizing a sophisticated code-switching skill alternating between formal and casual English, but have repeatedly been told to speak more "American" because of how language hierarchies positioned European languages as prestigious while treating Arabic and other languages spoken by Muslim students as obstacles to overcome.

Implementation Idea: Having a Linguistic Repertoires approach transforms this dynamic by treating all languages as valuable components in students' communicative toolkit. Rather than viewing languages as separate systems, this approach helps students recognize their complete linguistic resources and how different contexts activate different aspects of their language knowledge. In practice, this might include encouraging students to incorporate words from heritage languages when English equivalents don't capture full meanings—like using Arabic terms such as "tawakkul" (reliance on God while taking necessary action) that express concepts without direct English translations. During vocabulary instruction, exploring etymology across language families can also highlight how Arabic has influenced English and Spanish, positioning Muslim students' linguistic knowledge as valuable cultural capital. This approach doesn't require specialized training, just recognition that multilingual abilities represent sophisticated communication capacity rather than fractured English. When classroom environments normalize linguistic diversity through multilingual resources, displays, and discussions, Muslim students' linguistic knowledge becomes an asset rather than a liability.

Strategy 2: Rethinking Assessment: Beyond White Western Demonstration

Assessment practices often privilege particular ways of demonstrating knowledge that align with white Western traditions, potentially undervaluing the knowledge of students from different cultural backgrounds. For instance, physical education assessments might measure individual performance in isolated skills while missing competencies in teamwork, sustained endurance, or cultural movement forms where many of your minoritized students may excel. The key insight is recognizing that how we measure learning is culturally constructed and often our assessments are conforming to just one way of knowing that holds valuable or perceived as the standard, hence standardization in assessments. Multiple assessment pathways don't lower standards; they raise them by requiring students to demonstrate deeper understanding through methods that honor diverse ways of knowing and communicating.

Implementation Idea: Having a multiple pathways assessment approach addresses this disconnect by providing various routes for students to demonstrate understanding. A portfolio system might allow students to document physical competencies through traditional skills tests alongside video documentation of cultural movement forms, personal improvement tracking, and reflective analysis.

Strategy 3: Integrating Islamic Intellectual Traditions Across the Curriculum

Most curricula present Islamic intellectual traditions as historical artifacts confined to the golden age of medieval Islam, creating the impression that Muslim contributions belong to the distant past rather than ongoing knowledge traditions. Integrating Islamic intellectual traditions throughout curriculum challenges this historical quarantining. When teaching optics, exploring how Ibn al-Haytham's experimental method influenced the development of scientific processes creates direct connections between medieval Islamic approaches and contemporary practices. During environmental studies, incorporating Islamic environmental ethics alongside Western frameworks positions multiple knowledge systems as valuable approaches to sustainability questions. This integration extends naturally across subjects. History courses can present civilizations as interconnected knowledge systems rather than sequential chapters, tracing ongoing exchanges across geographic boundaries. Literature classes might explore diverse poetic traditions, examining how ghazal and sonnet forms approach structure and metaphor differently. The key is presenting Islamic intellectual traditions as continuous and evolving rather than frozen in time connecting historical contributions to ongoing knowledge development and contemporary applications. This approach challenges the property value of white Western knowledge by positioning multiple knowledge systems as academically legitimate.

Implementation Idea: Begin by evaluating one content area is your curriculum and determining how it can be made more inclusive and representative of the students in our classrooms. You've seen in the samples above how this can occur in virtually any subject area.

School-Wide Implementation

Meaningful change extends beyond individual classrooms when teachers strategically influence broader school culture.

Without waiting for administrative mandates or formal diversity initiatives, educators can collaborate to challenge whiteness as the institutional default through targeted approaches.

Teacher-Led Cultural Audits

The physical and cultural environment of schools often normalizes whiteness in subtle manifestations. Teacher study groups can examine these patterns by conducting informal cultural audits—walking through buildings with fresh eyes to identify whose images appear on walls, what assumptions shape school calendars, which foods get labeled as ethnic versus unmarked standard options, and how religious practices are accommodated or marginalized in physical spaces. These audits are useful because they can help reveal institutional patterns without targeting individuals. Teachers document where Western cultural practices are treated as neutral while Muslim practices are positioned as exceptions requiring special accommodation. They note which celebrations become school-wide events and which remain confined to multicultural units. They examine how school communications discuss religious observances—whether Christian holidays are simply holidays while Islamic observances require explanations or justifications. You might have noticed this in your own districts as petitions around changes to school calendars come up. In many districts most holidays of minoritized individuals are not given off, rather have to be requested as personal days off or religious observances.

What distinguishes this approach from traditional equity work is its teacher-centered nature. Rather than creating formal committees or comprehensive initiatives, teachers focus on making immediate changes within their sphere of influence. Teachers update classroom decorations, adjust department vocabulary, redesign events, and modify routines. These incremental changes often spread organically as other staff notice their impact on student engagement and belonging, creating gradual transformation without triggering the defensive reactions often associated with formal diversity mandates, and in that way lead to faster, longer-lasting results.

Collaborative Knowledge System Revision
The privileging of white Western knowledge is deeply embedded in curriculum structures, often positioning Islamic intellectual traditions as historical artifacts rather than ongoing knowledge systems. Cross-disciplinary teacher collaborations can challenge these hierarchies through focused examination of how subject areas encode assumptions about what knowledge counts. Teachers across departments might form informal study groups examining how their disciplines treat knowledge production across cultures. Science and history teachers explore how scientific achievements are attributed and contextualized, language arts and social studies teachers analyze whose literary traditions are centered, and math and art teachers investigate how cultural contexts shape creative expression. These collaborations identify specific points where curriculum could acknowledge multiple knowledge traditions as equally legitimate intellectual approaches rather than positioning Western frameworks as universal while treating others as supplementary.

The collaborative process suggested here naturally produces teaching resources that highlight Islamic scholars' ongoing contributions across disciplines, intentionally connecting historical figures to contemporary work. These teacher-led initiatives focus on questioning frameworks rather than simply adding diverse names to existing structures.

Conclusion

The stories we've examined, from kindergarten pronunciation lessons to high school college prep, reveal how thoroughly white cultural norms have embedded themselves as educational norms. When we mistake these norms for neutral standards, we transform education into a system that rewards proximity to whiteness while penalizing authentic expressions of Muslim identity and knowledge. We are bound to interrogate our most basic assumptions about what counts as academic, professional, or appropriate. It means recognizing that when we tell students their names are "too difficult," their languages lack prestige, or their cultural expressions seem unprofessional, we're enforcing a property system that has never been neutral.

The transformation happens in accumulated moments: when teachers invest time in pronunciation rather than defaulting to anglicized versions, when schools apply consistent standards to all political discourse rather than selectively silencing Muslim voices, when professional appearance policies reflect diverse cultural expressions rather than enforcing a single aesthetic norm. These shifts redistribute educational access by dismantling the assumption that white ways of being represent universal standards. Muslim students shouldn't have to choose between academic success and authentic self-expression. Creating educational environments where diverse forms of cultural capital are recognized and valued requires sustained attention to how our institutions have been shaped by and continue to privilege whiteness as an organizing principle.

Resources for Teachers and School Leaders

Academic and Professional Development Resources

- Harris, C. I. (1993). Whiteness as property. *Harvard Law Review*, 106(8), 1707–1791.
- Leonardo, Z. (2002). The souls of white folk: Critical pedagogy, whiteness studies, and globalization discourse. *Race Ethnicity and Education*, 5(1), 29–50.
- Yosso, T. J. (2005). Whose culture has capital? A critical race theory discussion of community cultural wealth. *Race Ethnicity and Education*, 8(1), 69–91.
- Said, E. W. (1978). *Orientalism*. Pantheon Books.

Curriculum and Instructional Resources

- Muslim Contributions to Civilization series (Islamic Networks Group)—Educational materials on Muslim contributions to various fields

- Decolonizing the Curriculum Network: Resources for integrating diverse knowledge traditions
- Zaytuna College: Resources on Islamic intellectual traditions for educators

School Policy and Implementation Guides

- National Equity Project: "Leading for Equity" implementation framework
- NYU Metro Center: "Culturally Responsive-Sustaining Education Framework"
- Islamic Networks Group: "Accommodating Muslim Students" guide for schools
- Mid-Atlantic Equity Consortium: "Equity Audit" tools for schools

Resources for Students

- "Ms. Marvel" graphic novels by G. Willow Wilson (Marvel Comics)
- "Love From A to Z" by S. K. Ali (Salaam Reads)
- "All American Muslim Girl" by Nadine Jolie Courtney (Farrar, Straus and Giroux)
- "Internment" by Samira Ahmed (Little, Brown Books for Young Readers)

7

The Essential Role of Allies

"Nobody's asking, 'hey, how are you doing. Is everything all right?'" —Rumaisa

Introduction

It was simple, but when Diana offered that she was there if I wanted to go for a walk, it felt like a gift I hadn't asked for. I used to love walking on trails by myself; until it was no longer safe to do so in the socio-political climate in our country. Standing at the intersections of multiple minoritizations often represents itself not in the spotlight moments, but in the ones that are mundane—the small things that are taken away, like teaching our boys to maintain a friendly tone and have their phone camera ready if they are ever asked to pull over, or looking for symbols of solidarity in professional and public spaces. In a political space where being vocal brings tremendous risk, being Muslim, in many ways, means always looking for allies for survival, that one person who may be just a silent supporter can be a source of great relief. Whether it's all the allies that rallied protesting the illegal arrest of Mahmoud Khalil, or people from all walks of life coming together for the Zohran Mamdani campaign, or the teacher who offers the Muslim high school student his classroom to pray in at Dhuhr time, allies are essential to uplifting the Muslim experience. In all the interviews I have done over the years with Muslim students this is a recurring theme: that one friend, that one afterschool club, that one teacher made all the difference.

The final tenet of MusCrit emphasizes that creating meaningful change for Muslim students requires more than individual effort; it demands collective action through essential allyship. In today's climate, where Muslim students face increasing surveillance, political targeting, and unprecedented levels of anti-Muslim racism, allies play a critical role in sharing the burden of advocacy while amplifying Muslim voices without appropriating their experiences. Allyship represents more than performative gestures or temporary solidarity. In the quote above, we see how Rumaisa felt unseen and unsupported at a time when her entire community was in dire distress. True allies engage in sustained action, educate themselves about Muslim experiences, intervene when witnessing anti-Muslim racism, and leverage their privilege to create institutional change all while following the lead of the Muslim communities they support. I will say though that many time allies fear coming across as politically incorrect when it comes to reaching out or coming from a place of curiosity. When that happens, choosing silence is never the better choice, stating your uncertainty and empathy as you lean in is.

For educators, becoming effective allies means going beyond trending cultural competence to developing specific understanding of the challenges facing Muslim students. It requires examining their own biases, learning about diverse Muslim experiences, cultivating classroom environments that challenge anti-Muslim bias, and advocating for institutional policies that support Muslim students' full participation in educational life. This chapter explores the multifaceted nature of allyship in educational contexts, examining both the responsibilities of allies and the strategies for effective coalition-building.

Framing our Conversation

The concept of solidarity, as articulated by Bell Hooks (1994), provides a foundation for understanding allyship not as charity but as mutual liberation. Hooks reminds us that authentic solidarity requires recognizing interconnected struggles against systems of oppression. For educators, this means understanding that creating educational environments where Muslim students can thrive benefits all students by challenging dehumanizing systems that ultimately harm everyone.

Freire (1970) would urge us to hold on to critical hope as we acknowledge the harsh realities in education spaces while maintaining our commitment to transformative possibilities. It's also important to note here Love's (2020) well-known distinction between allies and co-conspirators, offers additional perspective. While allies may support from positions of relative safety, accomplices take greater risks, using their privilege to disrupt oppressive systems. This might mean moving beyond classroom inclusion to advocating for institutional policy changes that face resistance, or publicly challenging Anti-Muslim practices even when doing so brings professional discomfort.

Reflective Practice

Think about what draws you to allyship work—is it personal connections to Muslim individuals, professional commitment to inclusive education, moral convictions about justice, or something else? Understanding these motivations helps clarify the sustainability of your allyship and potential blind spots that might limit its effectiveness. Also, think about your current relationship to Muslim communities. Do you have authentic connections with Muslim colleagues, students, or community members? Or is your understanding primarily theoretical? Effective allyship requires both intellectual understanding and relational connections.

Another critical piece to recognize is your comfort with discomfort, particularly in situations requiring intervention. When have you witnessed Islamophobia in educational spaces? How did you respond? What factors influenced your response: professional consequences, uncertainty about appropriate intervention, fear of making mistakes, or other considerations? Examine your institutional power and privilege. What specific forms of access, authority, or credibility do you possess that could be leveraged to support Muslim students? Identifying these resources clarifies your unique potential contribution to allyship work.

Finally, consider your sustainability as an ally. How are you balancing commitment to action with necessary self-care? What support systems help you maintain engagement with challenging issues? What boundaries do you need to establish to prevent burnout while remaining effectively engaged?

 Putting it into Action

Elementary Case Study: When Good Intentions Go Wrong

Mrs. Foster thought she was being helpful when she pulled Layla aside after math class. "Layla, I noticed you've been quieter lately. Is everything okay at home? I know sometimes families have... different expectations for girls."

Layla stared at her teacher, confused. "I'm fine. I was just thinking about the word problem."

"Oh! Good. I just wanted you to know that here at school, you can be anything you want to be. You don't have to you know, limit yourself."

Layla walked back to her desk wondering what her teacher meant. She'd never felt limited. She wanted to be a marine biologist, her parents encouraged her math skills, and she'd just been elected class representative. What was Mrs. Foster talking about?

The next day, during reading time, Mrs. Foster made an announcement. "Class, I've found some wonderful books about strong girls from different cultures. Layla, I think you'll especially like this one about a girl who becomes a doctor despite her family's traditions."

Layla accepted the book politely, but inside she cringed. Why was Mrs. Foster acting like her family held her back? This felt weird and uncomfortable.

At lunch, Layla mentioned the book to her friend Brandon. "My teacher keeps giving me books about girls who have to fight their families to succeed. It's annoying."

"That's stupid," Brandon said. "Your parents are like, the most supportive parents ever. Remember when you wanted to do the science fair project on ocean currents and your dad drove us to the coast three times?"

"Right? I don't get why she thinks I need rescuing."

The situation got weirder when Mrs. Foster started assigning Layla to work with Gabriela, the class's most outspoken student, "because Gabriela can help you practice speaking up." This confused everyone, including Gabriela.

"Layla speaks up plenty," Gabriela told her mom that evening. "She argued with Tyler about the Revolutionary War for like ten minutes yesterday. And she totally demolished his point about taxation."

Soon Mrs. Foster was hovering protectively whenever Layla interacted with male classmates, stepping in to "help" during perfectly normal conversations. When Layla was assigned to work with Alex on a science project, Mrs. Foster kept checking if Layla felt "comfortable" or needed to "switch partners."

"Mrs. Foster, I'm fine," Layla said after the third interruption. "Alex and I are just figuring out how to build the volcano." But Mrs. Foster continued treating Layla as if she were fragile, more gently than other students, as if she needed special protection from ordinary classroom interactions.

The awkward moment came during parent-teacher conferences. Layla's parents, both engineers who'd met in graduate school, listened as Mrs. Foster praised their daughter's courage in pursuing science despite cultural barriers.

"What cultural barriers?" asked Layla's father.

Mrs. Foster fumbled for words. "Well, I just assumed with your background... I wanted to make sure Layla knew she had options."

"What about our background suggests we don't support our daughter's education?" Layla's mother asked quietly.

Mrs. Foster realized she'd been making assumptions based on Layla's visible religious identity. She'd been trying to rescue a student who didn't need rescuing from a family that was already empowering her.

That evening, Layla's parents sat at their kitchen table trying to process what had happened. "She thinks we're oppressing our daughter," Layla's mother said quietly. "Should we say something? Request a different teacher?"

"I don't know. Will that make it worse for Layla? Will she be labeled as the family that complains?"

They sat in silence, weighing options that all felt inadequate. Speaking up might help Layla but could also mark her as different. Staying quiet might preserve peace but leave the underlying problem unaddressed.

The next morning, Layla came to breakfast with a question that surprised them. "Mom, Dad, why does Mrs. Foster act like you don't want me to be successful?" Her parents exchanged glances, realizing their daughter had been navigating this awkwardness alone while they'd been trying to figure out how to protect her from it.

Middle School Case Study: The Bathroom Revolt

The hateful messages appeared on a Tuesday. "TERRORISTS GO HOME" scrawled across the third stall in the girls' bathroom nearest the cafeteria. By Wednesday, someone had added "TOWEL HEADS" under it.

Khadija saw it first. She'd been having stomach problems all week; stress, probably, from the constant low-level tension that followed international news cycles. The bathroom vandalism made her feel nauseated in a new way. But, she didn't report it. What was the point? It would get painted over, and everyone would know she'd been the one to complain. Better to just avoid that bathroom.

But Thursday brought a problem: the bathroom closest to her locker was being repaired. The one near the gym required a hall pass during class. The cafeteria bathroom was the only convenient option.

Khadija held it through second period. Then third period. By fourth period, she was genuinely uncomfortable but still couldn't make herself go into that space.

Riley noticed her fidgeting during math class.

"You okay?"

"Fine," Khadija whispered, but she clearly wasn't.

At lunch, Riley watched Khadija avoid drinking anything and realized something was wrong.

"Seriously, what's going on?"

Khadija hesitated, then quietly told her about the graffiti.

Riley's response surprised her. "That's BS. We're going to deal with this."

"No, don't. It'll just make things worse."

"How could it be worse? You're dehydrating yourself because some **** wrote garbage on a wall."

After school, Riley went to investigate. She found the graffiti, took photos, and felt a surge of anger that surprised her with its intensity. This wasn't just mean; it was making her friend feel unsafe in their school.

But instead of reporting it to administration, Riley did something else. She texted the photos to her group chat with five other friends, adding, "This is in the bathroom by the cafeteria. Khadija's been avoiding it all week. This is not okay."

The responses came quickly: "What the hell?" "Who did this?" "This is disgusting." "We need to do something."

Tessa suggested they tell a teacher. Jordan wanted to stake out the bathroom to catch whoever was doing it. But Sage had a different idea.

"What if we just covered it up ourselves? Like, not painted over it, but covered it with other stuff?"

"What kind of stuff?"

"I don't know. Good stuff. Compliments. Jokes. Just... anything to make it not the first thing people see."

Friday morning, the six friends met before school with a stack of sticky notes and markers. They covered the offensive graffiti with dozens of small messages:

"You are enough." "Bad hair day? We've all been there." "Remember to drink water!" "Mrs. Peterson's test is gonna be rough. You got this!" "Your outfit is cute!"

They didn't make it specifically about the anti-Muslim graffiti. They just created a wall of positivity that buried the hate.

Word spread quickly. Other students started adding their own notes. By the end of the week, the entire bathroom was covered with encouraging messages, study tips, inside jokes, and general silliness.

But Monday brought a new problem. The custodial staff, following standard procedure, had removed all the sticky notes over the weekend. The original graffiti was visible again, along with some new additions.

This time, it wasn't just Riley's friend group who was angry. Students who'd enjoyed the positive bathroom culture were furious that it had been destroyed.

"They took down all our nice stuff but left the racist stuff?"

"That's not right."

"We should do something."

What happened next was organic and unstoppable. Students started carrying markers and sticky notes. Every time offensive graffiti appeared, it was immediately covered with positive messages. Not by a formal anti-hate campaign, but by individual students who'd decided they weren't going to let their bathrooms be spaces of hostility.

The administration finally took notice when the phenomena spread to other bathrooms. Instead of shutting it down, Principal Williams made a surprising decision. She provided official bulletin boards in each bathroom and invited students to continue their positive message campaign in designated spaces.

The most meaningful change was smaller and more personal. Khadija knew that if it happened again, her classmates would cover it up. She wasn't facing the hate alone anymore and that the students had created their own system of solidarity that didn't require adult permission or formal programming. They'd learned to take care of each other in immediate, practical ways.

High School Case Study: The Walkout That Wasn't

The email arrived on a Sunday night. "Due to security concerns, tomorrow's planned student walkout regarding international events has been cancelled. Students participating in unauthorized demonstrations will face disciplinary action."

Nour stared at her phone. There hadn't been a planned walkout. She would have known—she was president of the Student Council, editor of the newspaper, and generally aware of any student organizing happening at Lincoln High.

Unless... she scrolled through social media and found the source. Someone had created a fake event page calling for Muslim students to walk out in support of terrorist agendas. The page had been shared hundreds of times before being reported and removed.

But the damage was done. The administration's email made it seem like Muslim students were actually planning something disruptive. Nour's phone started buzzing with texts from friends, family, and classmates, some supportive, some confused, some accusatory.

Monday morning felt different. Nour noticed teachers watching her more carefully. Classmates who usually said "hi" avoided eye contact. In the hallway, she overheard two seniors talking.

"I heard they're planning something during lunch." "Who's 'they'?" "You know. The Muslim kids."

Nour felt sick. She'd been at Lincoln for four years, had never been political beyond normal student government stuff, and suddenly she was being treated like a potential security threat.

During second period, she got called to the office. Principal Martinez was there with the school resource officer.

"Nour, we need to talk about today's planned activities."

"What planned activities?"

"The walkout. We know you're involved in student organizing."

"Mr. Martinez, I literally found out about this fake event the same time you did. There is no walkout. Someone made that up."

She showed them her phone, walked them through the fake social media page, explained how she'd spent Sunday night texting Muslim students to make sure they knew it was fabricated.

"So you're saying no Muslim students are planning to demonstrate today?"

"I'm saying there was never a real plan. Someone created a fake event to make it look like we were organizing something we weren't."

The resource officer looked skeptical. "But you can't speak for all Muslim students."

"No, but I can speak for the ones I know, and none of us are planning anything."

Principal Martinez seemed torn between belief and caution. "Well, we're going to need to monitor the situation carefully today."

"Monitor what situation? There's nothing to monitor."

But there was something to monitor, just not what they expected. By lunchtime, it became clear that the administration's response to the fake threat had created a real problem. Muslim students were being watched, questioned, and treated with suspicion based on something that had never existed.

Rashid approached Nour during lunch. "Three teachers asked me today if I was 'planning anything.' I didn't even know what they were talking about until someone showed me that fake post."

"Same. It's like they think we're all secretly coordinating something."

"This is so messed up. We're being treated like we're guilty of something we never even thought of doing."

That's when Ethan Rivera, senior class president and definitely not Muslim, sat down at their table uninvited.

"Hey, so I heard about the fake walkout thing. That's really screwed up."

"Yeah, it is."

"What if we actually did a walkout? Not for the fake reasons, but to protest how you guys are being treated over something that was literally made up?"

Nour looked at him skeptically. "That's... not how this works, Ethan."

"Why not? I'm tired of watching the administration panic over made-up problems while real problems get ignored."

"Because then it looks like we were planning something all along."

"No, it looks like students care about fairness."

Word of Ethan's idea spread through the school's social networks. By the end of lunch, a genuine student movement was forming—not the fake one someone had invented, but a real response to how Muslim students were being treated.

But Nour found herself in an impossible position. If she supported the walkout, it would seem to validate the administration's suspicions. If she opposed it, she'd be rejecting solidarity from classmates who wanted to stand up for her.

The solution came from an unexpected source: Mrs. Patterson, the school librarian who'd never been involved in any political issues.

"Nour, can I talk to you?"

"Sure."

"I've been watching what's happening today. The whole thing is ridiculous. You're being treated like you did something wrong when you're actually the victim of someone else's lie."

"I know. But I don't know what to do about it."

"What if instead of a walkout, we had a 'walk-in'? Everyone who wants to show support could gather in the library during lunch to work on homework together. Nothing disruptive, nothing that could be misinterpreted. Just... solidarity through studying."

It was perfect. Completely legal, clearly educational, and impossible to characterize as threatening.

The next day, during lunch, the library filled with students of all backgrounds doing homework together. No speeches, no signs, no drama. Just a quiet statement that they weren't going to let fake controversies divide their school community.

The administration couldn't object to students studying. The community couldn't complain about disruption. And Muslim students got to see that their classmates recognized the unfairness of the situation without anyone having to make grand gestures or risk disciplinary action.

 **Think About It!**

Questions for Reflective Analysis

1. Mrs. Foster's "protective" approach to Layla demonstrates how allies sometimes center their own comfort over the actual needs of Muslim students. How can allies distinguish between advocacy that serves their need to feel helpful versus advocacy that actually empowers Muslim students?
2. The middle school bathroom campaign succeeded because peers took immediate, practical action rather than waiting for adult permission or formal programs. What does this suggest about the difference between ally-driven initiatives versus Muslim student-led resistance that allies support?
3. In the high school case, Muslim students found themselves defending against accusations about events that never existed, while the administration's response created real surveillance and suspicion. How can allies help disrupt these cycles where Muslim students are presumed guilty until proven innocent?
4. Each case study required thinking beyond standard approaches—questioning personal assumptions, creative problem-solving, and strategic responses to manufactured controversies. How might you prepare yourself to be a more effective ally during unpredictable moments when Muslim students need support?

Classroom Strategies and Activities

Strategy 1: Everyday Moments of Solidarity

The most powerful allyship often happens in the smallest interactions, the moment a classmate shares their snack during Ramadhan, or when someone naturally includes the hijabi student in playground games. Young children possess an intuitive sense of fairness that, when nurtured, becomes the foundation for lifelong allyship. Elementary teachers can cultivate this natural inclination by creating "kindness detective" opportunities where students notice and document acts of inclusion they witness or perform. Rather than artificial role-playing scenarios, this strategy builds on authentic moments that arise organically in classroom life. When Maria sits next to Fatima during lunch instead of sitting with her usual friends, or when David asks Omar to explain his prayer beads during show-and-tell rather than staring curiously, these become teachable moments for expanding everyone's understanding of solidarity.

The approach works because it doesn't single out Muslim students as problems requiring solutions, but instead positions all students as potential allies capable of creating inclusive classroom communities. Teachers facilitate by providing language for describing what they observe: "I noticed how you made space for Zaynab when she needed to step out for prayer. That showed real thoughtfulness about her needs." This narration helps children recognize their positive impact while building vocabulary for allyship.

Project Implementation: Community Care Documentation. Students can maintain individual Care Chronicles, simple journals where they record weekly observations of classroom kindness, inclusion, and mutual support. These aren't assignments with prompts but spaces for documenting what they notice: "Hassan helped me with my math today even though some kids make fun of his name." "Aisha taught me how to say hello in Arabic and now we greet each other that way every morning." Monthly, the class reviews these chronicles together, identifying patterns and discussing what makes their classroom feel safe and welcoming. Students create collaborative Kindness Maps showing how care moves through their classroom community, literally mapping connections between classmates. These maps reveal both strengths and gaps in classroom inclusion leading to organic discussions about how everyone contributes to community belonging.

Strategy 2: Interrupting Harm with Courage

Middle schoolers navigate a social landscape where belonging feels precarious and peer approval carries enormous weight. This makes them particularly vulnerable to participating in exclusion while simultaneously possessing the developmental capacity for moral courage. Effective allyship at this level requires teaching specific skills for interrupting harmful behavior while managing the social risks that intervention might create. Rather than expecting students to become social justice advocates overnight, this strategy builds intervention capacity gradually through practice with increasingly challenging scenarios. Students learn to distinguish between situations requiring immediate adult intervention versus those where peer response is appropriate and safe. They develop a repertoire of responses—from humor that deflects harmful comments to direct statements that redirect conversations.

The strategy also acknowledges that middle schoolers often witness anti-Muslim bias in spaces where adults aren't present: hallways between classes, social media exchanges, or lunch table conversations. Teaching them to navigate these moments prepares them for the real social situations they'll encounter while avoiding the helplessness that comes from generic "tell an adult" advice when adults aren't available.

Project Implementation: Response Strategy Scenarios. Working in small, deliberately diverse groups, students develop response strategies for authentic situations they might encounter: What to do when someone makes a terrorist joke after a current events discussion; how to respond when classmates exclude a Muslim student from a social gathering; ways to support a friend facing anti-Muslim harassment online.

Each group creates detailed scenario-based guides that include: assessment questions (Is this situation safe for peer intervention?), multiple response options (from subtle redirection to direct confrontation), and recovery strategies (how to manage if your intervention doesn't go as planned). Groups test their strategies through carefully facilitated practice sessions, refining approaches based on what feels authentic and sustainable.

The project culminates in students creating a peer resource like a handbook, app, or video series that provides practical guidance for their school community. This resource becomes a living document, updated as students gain experience implementing their strategies and learn from real-world outcomes.

Strategy 3: Leveraging Privilege for Systemic Change

High school students possess sophisticated understanding of institutional power and often express frustration with injustices they observe but feel powerless to address. This strategy channels that energy into concrete advocacy that leverages whatever privilege students possess: social capital, family connections, institutional access, to create meaningful change for Muslim peers.

Unlike earlier grades where allyship focuses primarily on interpersonal relationships, high school allyship can engage with systemic issues: advocating for policy changes around prayer space or dietary accommodations, challenging Islamophobic content in curriculum materials, or addressing disciplinary disparities that affect Muslim students differently. This approach requires helping students identify their specific forms of influence while learning to center Muslim voices in advocacy efforts. The strategy carefully navigates the distinction between allyship and appropriation by requiring student advocates to work in genuine partnership with Muslim students and community members. Non-Muslim students learn to amplify rather than replace Muslim voices, using their privilege to create platforms and opportunities rather than speaking on behalf of others.

Project Implementation: Policy Advocacy Lab. Students form advocacy teams that combine Muslim and non-Muslim members, with non-Muslim students explicitly taking support rather than leadership roles. Each team identifies a specific policy or practice affecting Muslim students' educational experience—from dress code restrictions to Ramadhan accommodations to curriculum representation. Teams conduct research using multiple sources: policy analysis, surveys of affected students, interviews with community members, examination of comparable policies in other districts. Non-Muslim team members leverage their social capital to gather data from peers who might not feel comfortable sharing experiences with Muslim students directly, while Muslim team members guide the analysis and advocacy priorities.

The lab culminates in presenting policy recommendations to school administration, with non-Muslim allies using their perceived credibility to validate concerns raised by Muslim students. Throughout the process, teams document their coalition-building strategies, challenges encountered, and lessons learned about effective cross-cultural advocacy, creating resources for future student organizers.

School-Wide Implementation

Creating Institutional Protection in Hostile Climates

Effective school-wide allyship requires institutional commitment to protecting Muslim students, particularly during periods of heightened Islamophobia. This commitment must manifest in concrete policies and practices rather than mere statements of support. To this end, work towards developing comprehensive anti-harassment policies that specifically address religious-based bullying and discrimination. These policies should include clear definitions of prohibited behaviors, specific reporting procedures, transparent investigation protocols, and accountability measures for violations. Unlike generic anti-bullying policies, these approaches should explicitly acknowledge the particular forms of harassment Muslim students experience, including those related to prayer practices, dietary needs, religious attire, and political expression. Most likely, teachers in the school already possess deep understanding of how anti-Muslim bias manifests in daily school life, yet this knowledge rarely informs institutional decision-making. Schools can systematically capture and utilize teacher observations about Muslim students' experiences, transforming individual classroom insights into institutional wisdom. From cafeteria interactions to hallway dynamics to after-school activities, teachers have likely already noticed patterns of discriminatory practice and can contribute their expertise about which accommodations work seamlessly and which create unwanted attention, which curriculum choices resonate authentically and which feel tokenistic, which intervention strategies actually reduce tension and which escalate it. This approach positions teachers as the institution's primary source of expertise about inclusive practice rather than recipients of external diversity training. By systematically gathering and acting on teacher knowledge about effective Muslim student support, schools can develop more relevant approaches grounded in authentic classroom experience.

Now more than ever before it has also become essential to implement proactive safety planning for periods of heightened tension, such as after international conflicts involving Muslim-majority countries or during political campaigns featuring anti-Muslim rhetoric. These plans might include increased monitoring of common areas, additional counseling resources, temporary modifications to security procedures, and communication protocols for addressing community concerns. Develop these plans collaboratively with Muslim students and families to ensure they address actual rather than assumed needs.

In my practice I have noticed that a major pain point for Muslim students is reporting. They are unlikely to report harassment or discrimination because of its sensitive nature, not wanting to make a big deal, or are afraid of the implications afterwards. Establishing confidential reporting systems that allow students to document concerns without fear of exposure is therefore incredibly important. These systems should include multiple reporting pathways—such as anonymous tip lines, trusted adult networks, and peer reporting option, ensuring that students can choose approaches that feel safest for their circumstances. Also confirm that these systems include robust follow-up procedures so reports result in meaningful action rather than disappearing into administrative processes.

Another particularly relevant and difficult area to address is creating clear guidelines for supporting student activism while ensuring safety. These guidelines should protect students' rights to political expression while providing frameworks for responsible advocacy. Include protocols for addressing external pressures on student activists, managing media inquiries, responding to community backlash, and ensuring that Muslim students aren't disproportionately burdened with educational or advocacy responsibilities during tense periods.

Navigating Resistance While Sustaining Allyship
The most difficult part of being an ally is maintaining your commitment when others push back. I've watched passionate teachers retreat from Muslim student advocacy after facing community complaints, administrative pressure, or colleague resistance. The isolation can be crushing, especially when you're already stretched thin with regular teaching responsibilities. We are all fairly aware that resistance to Muslim inclusion takes predictable forms. Parents may frame your inclusive practices as "political indoctrination." Colleagues might dismiss your concerns as "making everything about race and religion." Administrators could warn you about "keeping controversial topics out of the classroom," as if Muslim students' existence is inherently controversial. The most insidious resistance comes wrapped in seemingly reasonable language: "We support all students equally" or "Let's focus on what unites us rather than what divides us." Understanding these patterns helps you respond strategically rather than defensively. When someone accuses you of "pushing an agenda," they're really expressing discomfort with challenging dominant narratives. When they say Muslim students "need to assimilate," they're revealing assumptions about whose culture counts as normal. Recognizing the underlying dynamics helps you address root concerns rather than getting trapped in surface arguments.

Developing a resilience that allows you to maintain your allyship practice despite ongoing opposition is critical. A strategic persistence that protects both your effectiveness and your wellbeing cannot be overlooked. Documentation becomes your protection. Keep records of parent conversations, administrative directives, and colleague interactions related to your inclusive practices. Not because you're planning to file complaints, but because having accurate records helps you respond to challenges professionally and protects you from mischaracterizations of your work. When someone claims you're "forcing religion into the classroom," your documentation of curriculum standards and educational objectives provides clear professional justification.

Another huge but necessary undertaking is building incremental support among colleagues. I recommend not beginning with the most resistant teachers; focus on those who are genuinely curious or privately supportive but hesitant to speak up. Share the positive outcomes from inclusive practices whether it's increased student engagement, a welcoming classroom vibe or parent feedback. These organic conversations often influence colleagues more effectively than formal presentations about diversity. Sadly, sometimes the strongest resistance can come from teachers who consider themselves progressive. They might resist specifically Islamic content while embracing other forms of diversity. These conversations require particular sensitivity because they involve people you might consider natural allies.

The emotional toll of sustained resistance can lead to advocacy burnout if you don't develop sustainable practices. You cannot carry the full weight of institutional change alone. Setting boundaries around your advocacy work, by recognizing when and how much of yourself is available, helps you maintain long-term effectiveness rather than burning out after one semester of intensive effort.

When facing organized community resistance, remember that you're not defending your personal choices but upholding professional educational standards. Inclusive education isn't a political position, even though it is increasingly framed like that, it's pedagogical best practice supported by decades of research. Framing your work within established educational frameworks (critical thinking, global citizenship, college readiness) provides professional grounding that's harder to dismiss as personal agenda.

Conclusion

The sixth tenet of MusCrit, the essentiality of allies, completes our framework by emphasizing that creating educational environments where Muslim students can thrive requires collective action that transcends individual efforts. Throughout this chapter, we've explored how effective allyship manifests across different educational levels, addressing both developmental considerations and context-specific challenges.

The essentiality of allies connects in intricate ways to the previous tenets of MusCrit. Effective allies recognize the systemic nature of oppression (Chapter 2) rather than treating Anti-Muslim racism as isolated incidents. They understand the pivotal role of identifiability (Chapter 3) and provide support that addresses the specific vulnerabilities created by visible Muslim identity. They acknowledge the central role of gender (Chapter 4) by considering how Islamophobia impacts Muslim students differently across gender expressions and they amplify counter-narratives (Chapter 5) rather than speaking for Muslim students or reinforcing dominant representations. Finally, allies challenge whiteness as property and norm (Chapter 6) by recognizing and validating diverse forms of cultural knowledge and expression.

The current sociopolitical climate makes this work particularly urgent. As Muslim students navigate unprecedented levels of surveillance, political targeting, and hostility, allies play crucial roles in sharing advocacy burdens, providing institutional protection, and creating spaces where authentic expression remains possible despite external pressures. The strategies and case studies presented throughout this chapter provide concrete approaches for this work—from developing ally literacy and intervention skills, to building coalitions across difference, to creating institutional protections, to sustaining advocacy beyond critical incidents.

Resources for Teachers and School Leaders

Academic and Professional Development Resources

- Maira, S. (2018). *The 9/11 generation: Youth, rights, and solidarity in the war on terror*. NYU Press.
- Bayoumi, M. (2015). *This Muslim American life: Dispatches from the war on terror*. NYU Press.
- Council on American-Islamic Relations (CAIR). Annual Bullying Reports and Educational Resources.
- American Civil Liberties Union (ACLU): "Students' Rights: Religion and Public Schools" guides.

Curriculum and Instructional Resources

- Teaching Tolerance/Learning for Justice: "Religious Freedom" curriculum resources
- Facing History and Ourselves: "Standing Up for Democracy" unit with lessons on religious freedom and civil liberties
- Muslim Anti-Racism Collaborative (MuslimARC): Resources on allyship and coalition-building
- Institute for Social Policy and Understanding (ISPU): Educational materials on Muslim American experiences

School Policy and Implementation Guides

- ACLU: "Know Your Rights: Student Protests and Political Speech" guide
- Islamic Networks Group (ING): "Bullying Prevention Guide" for schools
- Religious Freedom Center: Implementation guides for protecting religious expression in public schools

Resources for Students

- Muslim Youth Voices Project: Platform for Muslim youth to share their stories and perspectives
- ACLU: "Student Rights Handbook" with specific guidance on religious freedom and political expression
- Jalali, R. (2010). *Moon watchers: Shirin's Ramadan miracle.* Tilbury House Publishers. (Middle grade novel exploring themes of identity and belonging)
- Ahmed, S. (2019). *Internment.* Little, Brown Books for Young Readers. (Young adult dystopian novel exploring civil liberties and Muslim American experiences)

Conclusion: The Work That Remains

This work is hard. It urges you to see systems you may have never questioned, to hear experiences previously unconsidered, and to act in ways that might make you uncomfortable.

When I started this book, I told you about my son calling himself Kevin in high school, about praying with the lights off in college, about making myself small in doctoral seminars. I shared these stories not seeking sympathy or to tell you a story of sorrow and resilience, but to help you understand that the students in your classroom are navigating impossible choices every day. They're calculating risks many never have to consider.

But I also want you to consider this: the Muslim experience is also one of joy. Let this text not lead you to a one-dimensional viewpoint. We emphasize the challenges so they can be addressed, but we must also be cautious that we don't compartmentalize the complete human experience in a way that leaves us thinking of full human beings only in parts, those parts that struggle. When I see Muslim students, yes, I see the worry, the double-take when they see themselves represented, but I also see them being silly, having inside jokes, celebrating Eid in full color, feeling hungry in Ramadhan only to stuff themselves at sunset. I see them weighed under the news of the world and then also get excited over five extra minutes of recess or a free ice cream sundae. I see many sharing stories of refuge and immigration, but many more sharing stories of BBQs and visits to the park. As we wrap up this reading, let's begin here. Let's begin by seeing these students as whole.

What We've Learned, What We Face

Through these chapters, we've examined how anti-Muslim racism operates in educational spaces, from the subtle erasure of Muslim history to the hypervisibility that makes daily prayer feel dangerous. We've seen how white cultural norms masquerade as universal standards, how counter-narratives get silenced, and how even well-meaning allies can center their own comfort over Muslim students' actual needs. We've also seen transformation. We've watched elementary teachers learn to pronounce names correctly and seen how that simple act can change a child's relationship with their identity. We've observed middle schoolers create organic solidarity movements and high school students develop critical media literacy that serves them beyond the classroom. This is the evidence of what becomes possible when educators commit to authentic change.

The Resistance You'll Face

Yes, you will have parents, colleagues, administrators and policy makers suggest that you are overstepping, overreacting, and overaccommodating. You will sense their disgruntlement and sometimes open hostility as well. You will also see discrepancy in the way people may support anti-racist work in other contexts, but vehemently oppose it in this. Most of this resistance is seated in fear and lack of knowledge, and we know that we cannot change hearts if there is no trust. Do your work, build your network, and others will follow. And when they don't, know that the students still saw you.

The Urgency of This Moment

I'm writing this conclusion during a time when Muslim students face unprecedented levels of surveillance, political targeting, and community hostility. University students are being doxxed for campus activism. High school students are self-censoring their political views to protect future college prospects. Elementary students are processing news about their communities that no child should have to navigate alone.

This isn't a moment for measured, gradual change. Muslim students need advocates now. They need educators who understand the particular vulnerabilities created by their hypervisible identities. They need allies who will speak up when they witness discrimination, even when doing so brings professional discomfort.

The work we do in schools today shapes how the next generation understands difference, belonging, and justice. When we fail to address anti-Muslim racism in educational spaces, we're not just harming Muslim students—we're teaching all students that some forms of discrimination are acceptable, that some voices don't matter, that some belonging is conditional.

But perhaps most importantly, success looks like educational environments where difference is engaged rather than erased, where difficult conversations happen regularly rather than being avoided, and where all students develop the critical thinking skills they need to navigate an interconnected world. In the appendices that follow, you'll find the practical tools to begin implementing MusCrit principles immediately. These aren't suggestions for someday, they're frameworks for the classroom you walk into tomorrow.

You're here, now. That's real talk.

Appendix A: Your Personal Journal

You don't need to master all six tenets before beginning this work. Start where you are, with what resonates most, and let your understanding deepen over time. The Muslim students in your classroom need you to begin, not to be perfect.

Where Are You Now? A MusCrit Self-Assessment

Before moving forward, take a moment to honestly assess your current practice. This isn't about judgment, it's about clarity on where you are and where you want to grow.

Recognizing Systemic Oppression

- [ ] I can identify examples of how Muslims are stereotyped in curriculum materials
- [ ] I understand how school policies might inadvertently disadvantage Muslim students
- [ ] I see patterns of discrimination beyond individual incidents
- [ ] I connect current Muslim experiences to historical context

Addressing Identifiability

- [ ] I create space for Muslim students to practice their faith (prayer, fasting, etc.)
- [ ] I respond appropriately when Muslim students face comments about their appearance
- [ ] I include visibly Muslim individuals in classroom examples and materials

- ◆ [ ] I understand the daily navigation required for identifiably Muslim students

Acknowledging Gender

- ◆ [ ] I move beyond stereotypical assumptions about Muslim women and men
- ◆ [ ] I include diverse Muslim gender experiences in my curriculum
- ◆ [ ] I understand how gender and Muslim identity intersect differently for each student
- ◆ [ ] I create space for Muslim students to express their gender identity authentically

Amplifying Counter-Narratives

- ◆ [ ] I include books and materials by Muslim authors in my classroom
- ◆ [ ] I create opportunities for Muslim students to share their perspectives
- ◆ [ ] I critically examine how Muslims are portrayed in curriculum materials
- ◆ [ ] I seek out authentic Muslim voices rather than stories about Muslims

Challenging Whiteness as Norm

- ◆ [ ] I recognize when white cultural practices are treated as universal standards
- ◆ [ ] I validate diverse forms of cultural knowledge and expression
- ◆ [ ] I examine my own assumptions about what counts as "academic" or "professional"
- ◆ [ ] I create space for multiple ways of knowing and being

Fostering Essential Allyship

- [ ] I speak up when I witness anti-Muslim bias or discrimination
- [ ] I educate myself about Muslim experiences rather than expecting Muslim students to educate me
- [ ] I build relationships with Muslim community members and organizations
- [ ] I advocate for Muslim students even when they're not present

Reflection: Which areas feel strongest for you? Which need the most attention? What patterns do you notice?

Quick-Start Implementation Checklist

Feeling overwhelmed? Start here. Pick 3–5 items that feel manageable for this week:

This Week I Will:

- [ ] Learn the correct pronunciation of all my Muslim students' names
- [ ] Examine one curriculum unit for stereotypes or missing Muslim perspectives
- [ ] Research one Muslim author to include in my classroom library
- [ ] Have a conversation with a Muslim student about their experience (if appropriate)
- [ ] Notice how I respond when Islam or Muslims come up in class discussions

This Month I Will:

- [ ] Attend one community event or presentation by a Muslim organization

- [ ] Review my classroom rules and procedures for unintentional bias
- [ ] Add one book by a Muslim author to my reading list or curriculum
- [ ] Connect with one colleague about creating more inclusive practices
- [ ] Examine how Muslim students are represented in my classroom materials

This Semester I Will:

- [ ] Implement one new strategy from each MusCrit tenet
- [ ] Build a relationship with a local Muslim community organization
- [ ] Advocate for one policy change that would benefit Muslim students
- [ ] Document the impact of my inclusive practices on student engagement
- [ ] Share my learning with other educators in my school

This Year I Will:

- [ ] Complete a full audit of my curriculum for Muslim representation and bias
- [ ] Develop expertise in at least one area of Muslim American history or culture
- [ ] Mentor another educator in implementing inclusive practices
- [ ] Engage with parents and community members about inclusive education
- [ ] Contribute to systemic change in my school or district

Questions for Deep Reflection

As you continue this journey, return to these questions regularly. Your answers will evolve as you grow:

About Your Practice:

- What assumptions about Muslim students have you had to examine and revise?
- How has your understanding of inclusive education changed through this work?
- What has surprised you most about implementing MusCrit principles?
- Where do you still feel uncertain or need more learning?

About Your Students:

- How do you see Muslim students differently now than when you started?
- What changes have you noticed in Muslim students' engagement or comfort?
- How have other students responded to more inclusive practices?
- What do you still need to understand about your students' experiences?

About Your Community:

- Who are your allies in this work, and how can you strengthen those relationships?
- What resistance have you encountered, and how are you navigating it?
- How has your school's climate changed as you've implemented these practices?
- What systemic changes does your school or district still need?

About Yourself:

- What has this work taught you about yourself as an educator?
- How do you sustain your commitment when the work feels challenging?
- What gives you hope about the future of inclusive education?
- How will you continue growing in your practice?

Appendix B: Classroom-Level Audit Tool

Instructions: Complete this audit 2–3 times per year to track your progress in creating inclusive environments for Muslim students. Rate each item using the scale below, then use the reflection questions to plan next steps.

Rating Scale:

- **4—Consistently Implemented**: This is embedded in my regular practice
- **3—Often Implemented**: I do this regularly but not consistently
- **2—Sometimes Implemented**: I do this occasionally when I think about it
- **1—Rarely Implemented**: I've tried this once or twice
- **0—Not Yet Implemented**: This is not part of my current practice
- **N/A—Not Applicable**: This doesn't apply to my teaching context

TENET 1: Recognizing Systemic Oppression

Practice	Rating	Notes
I examine my curriculum materials for stereotypes or biased representations of Muslims	___/4	
I can identify examples of how current events or policies might impact my Muslim students	___/4	
I understand how school policies (dress code, food service, holiday calendar) might affect Muslim families	___/4	
I recognize patterns of discrimination beyond individual incidents	___/4	
I connect current Muslim American experiences to historical context in my teaching	___/4	
I address misconceptions when they arise rather than ignoring them	___/4	

Subtotal: ___/24

TENET 2: Addressing Identifiability

Practice	Rating	Notes
I know which of my students observe Islamic practices (prayer, fasting, etc.)	___/4	
I provide appropriate time and space for Muslim students' religious observances	___/4	
I include visibly Muslim individuals in my examples, images, and materials	___/4	
I respond supportively when Muslim students face comments about their appearance or practices	___/4	
I understand the daily navigation required for students with visible Muslim identity	___/4	
I create classroom environments where religious expression is normalized	___/4	

Subtotal: ___/24

TENET 3: Acknowledging Gender

Practice	Rating	Notes
I avoid stereotypical assumptions about Muslim women and men	___/4	
I include diverse representations of Muslim gender experiences in my curriculum	___/4	
I understand how gender and Muslim identity intersect differently for each student	___/4	
I create space for Muslim students to express their authentic identities	___/4	
I address gender-based harassment or discrimination when it occurs	___/4	
I recognize and validate diverse Muslim perspectives on gender roles	___/4	

Subtotal: ___/24

TENET 4: Amplifying Counter-Narratives

Practice	Rating	Notes
I include books and materials by Muslim authors in my classroom	___/4	
I create opportunities for Muslim students to share their perspectives	___/4	

Practice	Rating	Notes
I critically examine how Muslims are portrayed in required curriculum materials	___/4	
I seek out authentic Muslim voices rather than stories about Muslims by non-Muslims	___/4	
I help students develop critical media literacy about Muslim representation	___/4	
I validate Muslim students' knowledge and experiences as classroom resources	___/4	

Subtotal: ___/24

TENET 5: Challenging Whiteness as Norm

Practice	Rating	Notes
I recognize when white cultural practices are treated as universal standards	___/4	
I validate diverse forms of cultural knowledge and expression	___/4	
I examine my assumptions about what counts as "academic" or "professional"	___/4	
I create space for multiple ways of knowing and demonstrating learning	___/4	
I recognize and address my own cultural biases in assessment and evaluation	___/4	
I include diverse cultural perspectives as legitimate academic content	___/4	

Subtotal: ___/24

TENET 6: Fostering Essential Allyship

Practice	Rating	Notes
I speak up when I witness anti-Muslim bias or discrimination	___/4	
I educate myself about Muslim experiences rather than expecting students to educate me	___/4	
I build relationships with Muslim community members and organizations	___/4	
I advocate for Muslim students even when they're not present	___/4	

Practice	Rating	Notes
I collaborate with colleagues to create more inclusive school environments	___/4	
I engage with parents and families in culturally responsive ways	___/4	

Subtotal: ___/24

TOTAL SCORE: ___/144

Scoring Guide:

- **120–144**: You're implementing MusCrit principles consistently. Focus on maintaining practices and mentoring others.
- **96–119**: You're making strong progress. Identify 2–3 areas for focused improvement.
- **72–95**: You have a solid foundation. Choose one tenet to deepen over the next semester.
- **48–71**: You're beginning to implement inclusive practices. Start with strategies that feel most manageable.
- **24–47**: You're in the early stages. Focus on learning and implementing basics in 1–2 tenets.
- **0–23**: This is your starting point. Begin with professional development and basic awareness building.

Reflection Questions:

1. Which tenet shows your strongest implementation? How can you build on this strength?
2. Which tenet needs the most attention? What's one specific step you can take this week?
3. What barriers prevent you from implementing certain practices? How might you address them?
4. How have your Muslim students responded to the practices you have implemented?
5. What support do you need to continue growing in this work?

School-Wide Audit Tool

Instructions

This audit should be completed by administrative teams, equity committees, or school improvement teams to assess institutional practices supporting Muslim students. Gather input from multiple stakeholders including teachers, students, families, and community members.

Rating Scale:

- **4—Systematically Implemented**: This is embedded in our policies and practiced school-wide
- **3—Widely Implemented**: Most staff implement this regularly with administrative support
- **2—Partially Implemented**: Some staff implement this, but it's not systematic
- **1—Minimally Implemented**: Few staff implement this, limited administrative support
- **0—Not Implemented**: This is not part of our current institutional practice

INSTITUTIONAL POLICIES AND PRACTICES

School Climate and Culture

Practice	Rating	Evidence/Notes
Our mission/vision statements reflect commitment to supporting all students' religious identities	___/4	
We have clear, publicized policies prohibiting religious discrimination and harassment	___/4	
Our disciplinary policies are applied equitably regardless of students' religious identity	___/4	
We track and address incidents of religious-based harassment or discrimination	___/4	
Our school calendar acknowledges major Muslim holidays	___/4	
We provide appropriate spaces and times for Muslim students' religious observances	___/4	

Curriculum and Instruction

Practice	Rating	Evidence/ Notes
Our curriculum includes accurate, positive representations of Muslim experiences and contributions	___/4	
We audit textbooks and materials for anti-Muslim bias before adoption	___/4	
Teachers receive professional development on inclusive practices for Muslim students	___/4	
Our library includes diverse books by Muslim authors across grade levels	___/4	
We teach critical media literacy that addresses stereotypes about Muslims	___/4	
Our history and social studies curriculum includes Muslim American experiences	___/4	

Staffing and Leadership

Practice	Rating	Evidence/ Notes
Our staff reflects the religious diversity of our student population	___/4	
We have Muslim educators or staff members in visible leadership roles	___/4	
Our hiring practices actively seek candidates with cultural competency for diverse populations	___/4	
All staff receive training on religious accommodation and inclusive practices	___/4	
We have designated staff trained to support Muslim students facing discrimination	___/4	
Leadership demonstrates visible commitment to supporting Muslim students and families	___/4	

Family and Community Engagement

Practice	Rating	Evidence/ Notes
We have established relationships with local Muslim organizations and community leaders	___/4	
Our communication materials are culturally responsive to Muslim families	___/4	

Practice	Rating	Evidence/Notes
We provide interpretation services for families who need them	___/4	
Muslim families serve in leadership roles (PTA, school committees, advisory groups)	___/4	
We host events that welcome and celebrate Muslim families and culture	___/4	
Our family engagement strategies are informed by Muslim community input	___/4	

Student Support Services

Practice	Rating	Evidence/Notes
Our counselors are trained to understand Muslim students' unique experiences	___/4	
We have systems to support Muslim students during times of heightened tension or discrimination	___/4	
Our food service accommodates halal dietary requirements	___/4	
We provide appropriate accommodations during Ramadhan and other religious observances	___/4	
Our dress code policies respect religious expression while maintaining safety standards	___/4	
We offer Muslim student clubs, affinity groups, or prayer spaces	___/4	

Assessment and Accountability

Practice	Rating	Evidence/Notes
We disaggregate data by religious identity to identify achievement gaps or disciplinary disparities	___/4	
We regularly survey Muslim students and families about their school experiences	___/4	
We have systems to track and respond to reports of religious discrimination	___/4	
Our school improvement plans include specific goals for supporting Muslim students	___/4	
We conduct regular climate surveys that include questions about religious inclusion	___/4	
We report on our progress in supporting Muslim students to the broader community	___/4	

TOTAL SCORE: ___/144

Scoring Guide:

- **120–144**: Your school demonstrates systematic commitment to supporting Muslim students. Focus on sustainability and continuous improvement.
- **96–119**: Your school has strong foundations with some areas for growth. Develop action plans for lower-scoring areas.
- **72–95**: Your school is making progress but needs more systematic approaches. Focus on policy development and staff training.
- **48–71**: Your school has begun addressing these issues but needs significant development. Start with leadership commitment and basic policies.
- **24–47**: Your school is in early stages of creating inclusive environments. Begin with awareness building and community engagement.
- **0–23**: Your school needs comprehensive planning to support Muslim students. Start with needs assessment and stakeholder engagement.

Action Planning Questions:

1. What are our greatest strengths in supporting Muslim students? How can we build on these?
2. Which areas need immediate attention? What are the barriers to improvement?
3. What resources (time, funding, expertise) do we need to make meaningful changes?
4. How will we engage Muslim students, families, and community members in improvement efforts?
5. What professional development does our staff need to implement these practices effectively?
6. How will we measure progress and maintain accountability for this work?

Implementation Priority Matrix:

High Impact + Easy to Implement (Do First):

- Policy clarifications
- Staff training
- Resource acquisition

High Impact + Hard to Implement (Plan Carefully):

- Curriculum overhaul
- Staffing changes
- Community partnerships

Low Impact + Easy to Implement (Quick Wins):

- Environmental changes
- Basic accommodations
- Communication improvements

Low Impact + Hard to Implement (Do Last):

- Complex system changes
- Expensive initiatives

Next Steps:

1. Share results with stakeholders
2. Form implementation team
3. Develop a 90-day action plan
4. Identify funding and resources
5. Schedule follow-up audit in 6 months

Bibliography

Abdel-Fattah, R. (2005). *Does my head look big in this?* Pan Macmillan.

Abo-Zena, M. M., & Tabbah, R. (2017). Muslim American women in campus communities. *Journal of Muslim Mental Health*, *11*(1), 45–63.

Abu El-Haj, T. R. (2015). *Unsettled belonging: Educating Palestinian American youth after 9/11*. University of Chicago Press.

Ahmed, S. (2019). *Internment*. Little, Brown Books for Young Readers.

Ali, N. (2021). Towards MusCrit: Counter-narratives of Muslim American students. *The High School Journal*, *104*(4), 203–207.

Ali, N. (2022a). *Counter-narratives of Muslim American women: Creating space for MusCrit*. Brill.

Ali, N. (2022b). MusCrit: Towards carving a niche in critical race theory for the Muslim American experience. *International Journal of Research & Method in Education*, *45*(4), 343–355.

Ali, S. K. (2018). *Saints and misfits*. Salaam Reads.

Ali, S. K. (2019). *Love from A to Z*. Salaam Reads.

Amrani, L. (2017). The racialization of Muslim Americans post-9/11 and the persistence of American Indian racialization. *American Behavioral Scientist*, *61*(14), 1691–1709.

Barlas, A. (2002). *"Believing women" in Islam: Unreading patriarchal interpretations of the Qur'an*. University of Texas Press.

Bayoumi, M. (2008). *How does it feel to be a problem? Being young and Arab in America*. Penguin Press.

Bayoumi, M. (2015). *This Muslim American life: Dispatches from the war on terror*. NYU Press.

Bell, D. (1992). *Faces at the bottom of the well: The permanence of racism*. Basic Books.

Beydoun, K. A. (2018). *American Islamophobia: Understanding the roots and rise of fear*. University of California Press.

Bourdieu, P. (1986). The forms of capital. In J. Richardson (Ed.), *Handbook of Theory and Research for the Sociology of Education* (pp. 241–258). Greenwood.

Buchanan, N. T., & Settles, I. H. (2019). Managing (in)visibility and hypervisibility in the workplace: A theory of organizational visual identity management strategies. *Journal of Management, 45*(4), 1374–1406.

Cainkar, L. A. (2009). *Homeland insecurity: The Arab American and Muslim American experience after 9/11*. Russell Sage Foundation.

Chicago Sun-Times. (2023, October 16). Wadea Al-Fayoume, 6-year-old Palestinian-American boy, stabbed to death in Plainfield Township hate crime. *Chicago Sun-Times*.

Cisneros, S. (1991). *The house on Mango Street*. Vintage Books.

CNN. (2015, September 16). Muslim teen Ahmed Mohamed creates clock, shows teachers, gets arrested. https://edition.cnn.com/2015/09/16/us/texas-student-ahmed-muslim-clock-bomb

Council on American-Islamic Relations California (CAIR-CA). (2024). *Campus climate report 2024*. CAIR-CA.

Council on American-Islamic Relations Massachusetts (CAIR-MA). (2025). *Silenced voices: Examining bullying and Islamophobia in Massachusetts public schools*. CAIR-MA.

Crenshaw, K. (1989). Demarginalizing the intersection of race and sex: A black feminist critique of antidiscrimination doctrine, feminist theory and antiracist politics. *University of Chicago Legal Forum, 1989*(1), 139–167.

Crenshaw, K. (1991). Mapping the margins: Intersectionality, identity politics, and violence against women of color. *Stanford Law Review, 43*(6), 1241–1299.

CUNY CLEAR (Creating Law Enforcement Accountability & Responsibility). (2013). *Mapping Muslims: NYPD spying and its impact on American Muslims*. CUNY School of Law.

Delgado, R. (1995). *Critical race theory: The cutting edge*. Temple University Press.

Diouf, S. A. (1998). *Servants of Allah: African Muslims enslaved in the Americas*. NYU Press.

Du Bois, W. E. B. (1903). *The souls of black folk*. A. C. McClurg & Co.

Faruqi, R. (2015). *Lailah's lunchbox: A Ramadan story*. Tilbury House Publishers.

Freire, P. (1970). *Pedagogy of the oppressed*. Continuum.

Garner, S., & Selod, S. (2014). The racialization of Muslims: Empirical studies of Islamophobia. *Critical Sociology, 41*(1), 9–19.

Goffman, E. (1963). *Stigma: Notes on the management of spoiled identity*. Prentice-Hall.

Hammer, J. (2012). *American Muslim women, religious authority, and activism*. University of Texas Press.

Harris, C. I. (1993). Whiteness as property. *Harvard Law Review*, *106*(8), 1707–1791.

hooks, b. (1994). *Teaching to transgress: Education as the practice of freedom*. Routledge.

Jalali, R. (2010). *Moon watchers: Shirin's Ramadan miracle*. Tilbury House Publishers.

Kahf, M. (2003). *E-mails from Scheherazad*. University Press of Florida.

Khan, H. (2018). *Amina's voice*. Salaam Reads.

Kundnani, A. (2014). *The Muslims are coming! Islamophobia, extremism, and the domestic war on terror*. Verso Books.

Ladson-Billings, G., & Tate, W. F. (1995). Toward a critical race theory of education. *Teachers College Record*, *97*(1), 47–68.

Lahiri, J. (2003). *The namesake*. Houghton Mifflin.

Leonardo, Z. (2002). The souls of white folk: Critical pedagogy, whiteness studies, and globalization discourse. *Race Ethnicity and Education*, *5*(1), 29–50.

Love, B. L. (2019). *We want to do more than survive: Abolitionist teaching and the pursuit of educational freedom*. Beacon Press.

Love, B. L. (2020). Dr. Bettina Love explains what she means by a co-conspirator [Video clip]. C-SPAN. www.c-span.org/clip/public-affairs-event/user-clip-dr-bettina-love-explains-what-she-means-by-a-co-conspirator/4880307

Love, E. (2017). *Islamophobia and racism in America*. NYU Press.

Maira, S. (2018). *The 9/11 generation: Youth, rights, and solidarity in the war on terror*. NYU Press.

Mamdani, M. (2004). *Good Muslim, bad Muslim: America, the Cold War, and the roots of terror*. Pantheon Books.

Mir, S. (2014). *Muslim American women on campus: Undergraduate social life and identity*. University of North Carolina Press.

Muhammad, I., & Ali, S. K. (2019). *The proudest blue: A story of hijab and family*. Little, Brown Books for Young Readers.

MusCrit. (n.d.) www.muscrit.com

NPR. (2025, April 8). "Citizenship won't save you": Free speech advocates say student arrests should worry all. www.npr.org/2025/04/08/

nx-s1-5349472/students-protest-trump-free-speech-arrests-deportation-gaza

Peek, L. (2017). *Behind the backlash: Muslim Americans after 9/11*. Temple University Press.

Prince Among Slaves [Documentary]. (2007). Unity Productions Foundation.

Puar, J. K. (2007). *Terrorist assemblages: Homonationalism in queer times*. Duke University Press.

Rana, J. (2011). *Terrifying Muslims: Race and labor in the South Asian diaspora*. Duke University Press.

Saeed, A. (2018). *Amal unbound*. Nancy Paulsen Books.

Said, E. W. (1978). *Orientalism*. Pantheon Books.

Satrapi, M. (2000). *Persepolis: The story of a childhood*. Pantheon Books.

Sirin, S. R., & Fine, M. (2008). *Muslim American youth: Understanding hyphenated identities through multiple methods*. New York University Press.

Thobani, S. (2007). *Exalted subjects: Studies in the making of race and nation in Canada*. University of Toronto Press.

Thomas, J. M. (2010). The racial formation of medieval Jews: A challenge to the field. *Ethnic and Racial Studies, 33*(10), 1737–1755.

Wadud, A. (1999). *Qur'an and woman: Rereading the sacred text from a woman's perspective*. Oxford University Press.

Wilson, G. W. (2013). *Ms. Marvel series*. Marvel Comics.

Yosso, T. J. (2005). Whose culture has capital? A critical race theory discussion of community cultural wealth. *Race Ethnicity and Education, 8*(1), 69–91.

Zaal, M. (2012). Islamophobia in classrooms, media, and politics. *Journal of Adolescent & Adult Literacy, 55*(6), 555–558.

Zoboi, I. (Ed.). (2019). *Black enough: Stories of being young & Black in America*. Balzer + Bray.

Organizational Resources

American Civil Liberties Union (ACLU). Students' rights: Religion and public schools guides. www.aclu.org/

Asian Americans Advancing Justice. Resources addressing intersection of religious and racial discrimination. www.advancingjustice.org/

Constitutional Rights Foundation. Terrorism and security: Educational materials examining civil liberties and national security. www.crf-usa.org/

Council on American-Islamic Relations (CAIR). Educational resources and bullying reports. www.cair.com/

Electronic Frontier Foundation. Surveillance self-defense guide. https://ssd.eff.org

Facing History and Ourselves. Confronting Islamophobia: Teaching resources with sections on security policies. www.facinghistory.org/

HEART Women & Girls. Resources for Muslim girls on health and well-being.

Hijabi Ballers. Organization celebrating Muslim women in sports.

Islamic Networks Group (ING). Religious practices of Muslim students in public schools. https://ing.org

Learning for Justice. Responding to anti-Muslim bias. https://learningforjustice.org

Muslim Anti-Racism Collaborative (MuslimARC). Intersectional resources addressing gender and race. www.muslimarc.org/

Muslim Advocates. Legal resources and educational materials on civil rights issues affecting Muslim students. https://muslimadvocates.org/

Muslim Legal Fund of America (MLFA). Student rights guide. https://mlfa.org

Muslim Public Affairs Council (MPAC). Inclusion of American Muslims school guide. www.mpac.org/

National Association of Muslim Lawyers (NAML). Digital rights resources and legal referrals. https://naml.org/

National Education Association. Religious freedom in public schools resources. www.nea.org/

National Women's History Museum. Digital resources on women's contributions across cultural contexts. www.womenshistory.org/

NYU Metro Center. Culturally responsive-sustaining education framework.

PBS Learning Media. Collection of Muslim Journeys digital resources. www.pbslearningmedia.org/

Religious Freedom Center. Implementation guides for protecting religious expression in public schools. https://religiousfreedomcenter.org

Smithsonian Institution. America to Zanzibar: Muslim cultures near and far digital exhibition. www.si.edu/

Tanenbaum Center for Interreligious Understanding. Respecting religious identity in schools: Classroom strategies for addressing harassment. www.tanenbaum.org/

Teaching While Muslim. Supporting identifiable Muslim students: Classroom resources by Muslim educators. www.teachingwhilemuslim.org/

The Advocates for Human Rights. Energy of a nation: Immigrants in America curriculum with modules on post-9/11 policies. www.theadvocatesforhumanrights.org/

Unity Productions Foundation. Muslims and the making of America documentary and curriculum guide. https://upf.tv/

Yaqeen Institute for Islamic Research. Navigating Muslim identity in schools. https://yaqeeninstitute.org

Zaytuna College. Resources on Islamic intellectual traditions for educators.

For Product Safety Concerns and Information please contact our EU representative GPSR@taylorandfrancis.com
Taylor & Francis Verlag GmbH, Kaufingerstraße 24, 80331 München, Germany

www.ingramcontent.com/pod-product-compliance
Lightning Source LLC
Chambersburg PA
CBHW070808230426
43665CB00017B/2526